Get the eBook FREE!

(PDF, ePub, Kindle, and liveBook all included)

We believe that once you buy a book from us, you should be able to read it in any format we have available. To get electronic versions of this book at no additional cost to you, purchase and then register this book at the Manning website.

Go to https://www.manning.com/freebook and follow the instructions to complete your pBook registration.

That's it!
Thanks from Manning!

A Pythonic Adventure

FROM PYTHON BASICS TO A WORKING WEB APP

PAVEL ANNI

MANNING
SHELTER ISLAND

Manning Publications Co.
20 Baldwin Road
PO Box 761
Shelter Island, NY 11964

Development editor: Toni Arritola
Technical editor: Marie-Therese Smith
Review editor: Adriana Sabo
Production editor: Andy Marinkovich
Copy editor: Andy Carroll
Proofreader: Mike Beady
Typesetter: Gordan Salinovic
Cover designer: Monica Kamswaag

ISBN 9781633438897
Printed in the United States of America

For my Dad

brief contents

contents

preface

This book is based on a real story. My son, Erik, liked to go to Starbucks and try drinks with different flavors and toppings. One day, he decided to prepare drinks himself and treat his friends. He took his tablet to collect orders from them, but I suggested he create a simple program for that. He had tried to learn programming before, but most of the exercises were boring for him. This time, he saw a real problem he could solve with programming, and he got interested.

That's how this book was started. I hope you'll find your own interesting problem that can be solved with programming—and I hope this book will help you.

Here are a few pieces of advice:

- *Don't rush*—I understand your desire to go directly to the last chapter, download the code for the final version of the program, and run it. Don't do it. Go step by step, write the code yourself (don't copy and paste, please!), try it, and move forward. Sometimes, you may have to return and re-read a chapter. Sometimes, you'll need a break. Don't worry! Take a break and repeat the chapter—just don't drop out.

- *Make mistakes*—You don't learn when everything goes perfectly well. The only way to learn is to make mistakes. Don't be afraid of mistakes. Experiment with the code, change things, get error messages, and read them. Search for the error message on the internet, and discover thousands of other people who made the same mistake. Learn how they fixed it and then fix yours. Move ahead and don't drop out.

- *Ask questions*—Ask your friends, ask your parents and grandparents, ask the internet. Explain your problem to somebody—sometimes that's enough to figure out the solution yourself. There is no such thing as "stupid questions"—don't be shy. Ask questions and don't drop out.

- *Go further*—Modify the application you create with this book. Change something to make it look more like your own app. Think about other applications you can create. Look around you: what can be automated? Can you create an app that's similar to an app or a website you know? Tell your friends about your ideas—maybe you'll create something together. Programming is cool. Don't drop out.

- *Speak out*—Please share your experience in the liveBook discussion forum. Share your thoughts and ideas with friends. Discussing problems you have solved will make your own Pythonic adventure much more interesting.

acknowledgments

This is my first book, and I couldn't have written it without the invaluable support and guidance from numerous individuals.

First and foremost, I want to express my gratitude to my parents. My dad, a firm believer in the importance of STEM education, filled our home with popular science books and encouraged me to learn programming. He astutely predicted that it would become a second literacy, and he couldn't have been more accurate. My mom, a lifelong physics teacher, generously passed down her pedagogical genes to me.

I must also thank my sons, Simon and Erik, for providing me with the opportunity to teach them Python. That invaluable experience allowed me to learn and grow as both an educator and a programmer.

To my wife, Tatiana, I extend my heartfelt appreciation for her immense patience and unwavering support. She graciously endured many weekends when I focused on writing at the keyboard instead of enjoying her delightful company. Throughout the process, she listened to my thoughts and ideas, offering her invaluable advice and perspective.

My gratitude extends to my Manning editors: Troy Dreier, Toni Arritola, and Marie-Therese Smith, who played instrumental roles in bringing this book to fruition. Troy recognized the potential in my early draft and brought it to Manning for consideration, without which this book would never have been started. Toni's gentle yet persistent encouragement ensured the book's timely completion. Without her, this book would never have been finished. Marie-Therese, who has worked as an educator, engineer, and data scientist, meticulously tested the code and technical details, preventing readers from stumbling on the very first coding example.

I would like to acknowledge Nicholas H. Tollervey, the primary author of the Mu editor, and all the contributors to this fantastic open-source project. This beginner-friendly Python development environment provided everything I needed for this book's journey, from the first steps in Python to the development of a full-stack web application.

To all the reviewers: Afif Hayder, Al Pezewski, Alan Gil Forza, Alexis Perrier, Amogh Raghunath, Andrew R. Freed, Arsalan Khan, Arya ArunKumar, Jean-Baptiste Bang Nteme, Ben McNamara, Bernard Fuentes, Chris Kardell, Christian Sutton, Clara McAdams, Clemens Baader, David Kuhta, Dhivya Sivasubramanian, Elona Vialatte, Faiyaz Evan Hayder, Ganesh Swaminathan, George Thomas, Greg Freed, Hannah Cheung, Hasin Hayder, Jackson McNamara, Jana Dragosavljević, Janit Anjaria, Jimena de Jesús Mata Cobián, João Dinis Ferreira, Keith Kim, Kevin Cheung, Mafinar Khan, Marc-Anthony Taylor, Mary Anne Thygesen, Miguel Eduardo Gil Biraud, Nathan-Steven Taylor, Nik Piepenbreier, Ninoslav Čerkez, Or Golan, Pavel Šimon, Philippe Vialatte, Regina de Jesús Mata Cobián, Robert Kulagowski, Rupa Lahiri, Sataduru Roy, Shaurya Dara, Shivansh Batra, Shyon Roy, Sravanthi Reddy, Srisha Reddy, Srisha Thimmareddy, Sudeep Batra, Sumit Bhattacharyya, Tarun Ganesh, Tawhida Hussain, Walter Alexander Mata López, Will Pezewski, and Wolfie Baader, your suggestions helped make this a better book.

Last, I extend my heartfelt thanks to the entire Python community. The wealth of knowledge I've gained from podcasts, videos, conference talks, books, and online forums over the years is immeasurable. The welcoming and supportive nature of this community is undoubtedly a significant reason why Python is so cherished by developers. Thank you all!

about this book

I wrote this book for teenagers who want to learn programming via practical projects. In the book, you'll find a series of informal dialogues between two brothers working together on a Coffee Shop application. Follow their conversations and develop your own application along with them.

Who should read this book?

Maybe you have taken a programming class already—online or at school. You know the basics, but you haven't tried to create a real-life project yet.

Maybe you haven't started with programming yet, but you know how to use a computer, and you want to learn how programming works.

Maybe you have used some online applications, and you want to create your own.

Maybe your older brother or sister creates computer programs and applications already, and you want to learn programming too.

If any of the above are you—great! With this book, you'll learn step by step with Erik and Simon and create your own application in a couple of weeks.

If you're a (grand)parent, and you want an easy-to-follow guide to learning programming with your (grand)children, this book is for you too! Even if you want to learn programming yourself, don't think that this book is for kids only. Everybody is welcome to learn Python and create applications!

How this book is organized: A roadmap

Each chapter in this book covers what Erik and Simon (and later, Emily) created in one day. They sat together for about an hour each day, talked about their application, and wrote code. You can do the same—read a chapter a day and write the code for that chapter. If you have questions, ask them in the book's forum or search the internet.

There are 15 chapters in the book.

Part 1 consists of the first 9 chapters, where Erik and Simon work on the first version of their application, which is text based. That means it works like a chat, asking customers what they want to order and waiting for their answers.

In chapter 1, Erik gets the idea for his application. He wants to prepare coffee drinks for his friends, and he has to collect orders for them. Simon helps him create the first version of his application.

In chapter 2, Erik learns about lists. Lists are a good way to organize your menus with different kinds of flavors and toppings.

In chapter 3, Erik notices that he repeats his code several times. Simon suggests using functions to avoid that. The application code becomes shorter and easier to read.

In chapter 4, Erik and Simon work on user errors. What if a customer makes a mistake when entering their order? Your application should take care of that.

In chapter 5, Simon teaches Erik how to use files. Now the shop manager can edit text files to add or remove flavors or toppings from the menu.

In chapter 6, the brothers create a main menu for the application. That allows them to run the application continuously and serve one customer after another.

In chapter 7, Erik and Simon create more functions. They use functions to get the order and print it out.

In chapter 8, Erik learns about JSON. Simon explains how to use a JSON file to store the orders.

In chapter 9, the brothers finish the text-based version of the application. They discuss how to make a web-based version of it.

In part 2 (chapters 10–15), Erik, Emily, and Simon work on a web version of their application. They create web-based menus, connect a database, and work on styles and colors. Finally, they test their application on smartphones and tablets.

In chapter 10, Emily joins the brothers. Simon shows Emily and Erik how to create a very simple web application. They learn how to use web forms and menus.

In chapter 11, Emily and Erik work on creating web forms and menus for their coffee shop.

In chapter 12, Simon explains to Emily and Erik how to use databases to store orders. They learn how to use Structured Query Language (SQL) to do that.

In chapter 13, the friends start making their web application pretty. They learn how to use fonts, colors, and images on web pages.

In chapter 14, Simon shows Emily and Erik how to use artificial intelligence (AI) to improve their application code, write comments, and explain error messages.

In chapter 15, Emily, Erik, and Simon make the application available to their smartphones and tablets and test it. It works! They discuss their next steps: how to make the application available on the cloud and how to add more features to it. They decide to continue working on the application, but to use a website to exchange their ideas.

I suggest reading this book as a story, chapter by chapter. Please don't skip the parts marked as "YOUR TURN." You'll have to write the code that Erik, Emily, and Simon wrote, but in your own way. Use your imagination, change things, and create your own unique application! Sometimes, you'll want to take a break. Sometimes, you'll want to re-read a chapter to understand it better. That's okay. Go through the book at your own pace—just don't drop out!

If you're stuck on some piece of code, try to copy it from our code repository (discussed next). If something isn't clear, ask a question in the liveBook forum (discussed shortly).

About the code

The source code for this book can be found on GitHub: https://github.com/pavelanni/pythonicadventure-code. At the end of each chapter is a link to the code for that chapter. You can also get executable snippets of code from the liveBook (online) version of this book at https://livebook.manning.com/book/a-pythonic-adventure.

This book contains many examples of source code, both in numbered listings and inline with normal text. In both cases, the source code is formatted in a `fixed-width font like this` to separate it from ordinary text.

In many cases, the original source code has been reformatted; we've added line breaks and reworked indentation to accommodate the available page space in the book.

Additionally, comments in the source code have often been removed from the listings when the code is described in the text. Code annotations accompany many of the listings, highlighting important concepts.

liveBook discussion forum

Purchase of *A Pythonic Adventure* includes free access to liveBook, Manning's online reading platform. Using liveBook's exclusive discussion features, you can attach comments to the book globally or to specific sections or paragraphs. It's a snap to make notes for yourself, ask and answer technical questions, and receive help from the author and other users. To access the forum, go to https://livebook.manning.com/book/a-pythonic-adventure/discussion. You can also learn more about Manning's forums and the rules of conduct at https://livebook.manning.com/discussion.

Manning's commitment to our readers is to provide a venue where a meaningful dialogue between individual readers and between readers and the author can take place. It is not a commitment to any specific amount of participation on the part of the author, whose contribution to the forum remains voluntary (and unpaid). We suggest you try asking the author some challenging questions lest his interest stray! The forum and the archives of previous discussions will be accessible from the publisher's website as long as the book is in print.

Other online resources

The book has a companion site: https://pythonicadventure.com. On this site, we collected some ideas for other similar projects (in case you don't like the coffee shop project), troubleshooting information, and ideas for improving the application.

The best source for information about Python is the official site: https://www.python.org. You'll find all the necessary documentation, blogs, articles, and tutorials there. One of the most useful sites for beginners is this collection of links to other resources: https://wiki.python.org/moin/BeginnersGuide.

Going further

After finishing this book, you'll be ready to work with Python more seriously. Consider the following books as you continue your Pythonic Adventure:

- *Tiny Python Projects* by Ken Youens-Clark (https://www.manning.com/books/tiny-python-projects)
- *Python Workout* by Reuven M. Lerner (https://www.manning.com/books/python-workout)
- *Practices of the Python Pro* by Dane Hillard (https://www.manning.com/books/practices-of-the-python-pro)

about the author

PAVEL ANNI is a Principal Customer Engineer at SambaNova Systems. Before joining this AI startup, Pavel worked for Sun Microsystems, Oracle, and Red Hat. In his career, his main role has been training people and popularizing new technologies. He has developed and delivered courses on programming languages, the Unix and Linux operating systems, Kubernetes, and other topics.

Coffee for friends: First steps

It all started on a sunny summer day. Erik came home with an idea: he wanted to prepare coffee drinks for his friends. Who knew that he would create his own online application for that?

"I'll make it just like at Starbucks, with many flavors and toppings," he thought. "I think I have everything I need: coffee, three or four flavors to add, and some chocolate cream for toppings. Great!"

"Where's my iPad?" he asked his older brother Simon.

"Where you left it. Why?"

"I need it to collect orders for my coffee shop!"

He came back several minutes later with notes on his iPad, prepared four drinks for his friends, and left again.

"Wasn't it a good idea?" he asked Simon, when he came home with four empty plastic cups.

"Yes, great idea," Simon said. "But . . ."

"What '*but*'?" Erik asked. He felt that his older brother wanted to ruin his day—as he usually did.

"You used your iPad to take orders, but you used it just as a plain paper notepad. You could create a simple application for your coffee shop and use it to take orders."

"You mean, like in an online shop? With menus and all that?" Erik already imagined *his own* web store with a huge title at the top: "Erik's Coffee Shop."

"Yes, of course. You know a bit of Python from that online course you took, don't you?"

"Yes, but I don't remember much. We did some exercises . . . I think it will be difficult to make it look like a real online shop."

"Don't worry," Simon said. "We'll do it step by step. I did several projects like this for my robotics team at school."

NOTE Don't worry if you don't have *any* programming experience at all. Erik didn't remember much from his classes anyway, so we'll start at the very beginning.

Simon was in his last year of high school. He had learned Python several years ago and used it in the school's Computer Science Club and, more recently, on his robotics team.

"So you are saying we can build a real online application?" Erik was not convinced.

"Yes, sure. If you don't drop out from my class," Simon smiled, "you will build it in a couple of weeks. Then your customers will be able to choose whatever drink they want, add flavors . . ."

"And toppings!" Erik added.

"Yes, and toppings. And after they confirm the order, you'll see it on the orders page. You'll know what to prepare and for whom. Something like this," and Simon took a piece of paper and started to draw a simple web page. "This will be your order page.

"And this will be your list of orders."

"Cool! Do you think we can do it?" Erik still couldn't believe his brother.

"Of course! As I said, just don't drop out. You have plenty of time to finish it during your summer break."

NOTE   There are several other project ideas that you can use if you don't like the coffee shop idea. Some of them will be discussed when Erik's friend Emily joins him in later chapters. Look for more details in appendix A.

First things first: Installation

"Let's start with some simple things. You will remember Python very quickly. Do you have it installed on your laptop?" Simon asked.

"No, I don't think so."

"Here is a great Python editor, designed specifically for beginners like you. It's called Mu. Try to find it and install it. You can do it, I'm sure."

Erik found the website where he could download it: https://codewith.mu/.

He downloaded the installation program from the Download page: https://codewith .mu/en/download.

He clicked the Instructions button and found an instructions page with all the steps for his computer.

"Don't worry, it's not a toy. It's a perfect editor," Simon said. "We use it on our robotics team to work with microcontrollers. As you can see, there are versions for Windows, macOS, and Linux. I use the Linux version with my team."

NOTE You can find all the necessary links and instructions in appendix B.

Download   About   Tutorials   How to..?   Discuss   Developers   Language ▾

Download Mu

The simplest and easiest way to get Mu is via the official installer for Windows or Mac OSX (we no longer support 32bit Windows). We also have an experimental AppImage for Linux users running on Intel based hardware.

The current recommended version is Mu 1.2.0. We advise people to update to this version via the links for each supported operating system. All previous beta versions of Mu can be downloaded from here.

"Are there other editors for Python?" Erik didn't want to just follow his brother's directions.

"Yes, of course, many of them. Another good option for beginners is Thonny. Look here: https://thonny.org/."

"I like it!" said Erik. "And the name is funny."

"And, of course, there are other code editors that work on every platform:

- VS Code (https://code.visualstudio.com/)
- Sublime Text (http://www.sublimetext.com/)

"They all work perfectly with Python. Even the very old editors, like Vim (https://www.vim.org/) and Emacs (https://www.gnu.org/software/emacs/), support Python, but you have to be a *very serious* programmer to use them," and Simon winked at his brother.

"Mu and Thonny," Simon continued, "both *include* Python when you install them. To use Python with *other* editors, you have to *install* it first. On some systems, like Linux and macOS, Python is already installed from the beginning. On Windows, you'll need to install it. I can show you how later if you want."

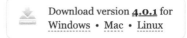

Your Turn!   Install your Python environment

Now it's your turn. Open your laptop or desktop and install the Mu editor. You can find the complete instructions for different platforms in appendix B (it's available for Windows, macOS, and Linux).

If you prefer some other editor, feel free to install it instead of Mu. Don't be afraid to experiment!

How to talk to a computer

"Let's start Mu and begin writing your coffee shop program," Simon said.

Erik launched Mu and saw its first window.

"Select Python 3 from the menu and click OK," Simon suggested.

Erik did what Simon said. "From now on," Simon continued, "Mu will remember that you prefer to use Python 3. Maybe you noticed that there are some other modes that can be used to work with microcontrollers, build web applications, and do other things. But for now, we need only the Python 3 mode."

Now Erik had the editor window in front of him.

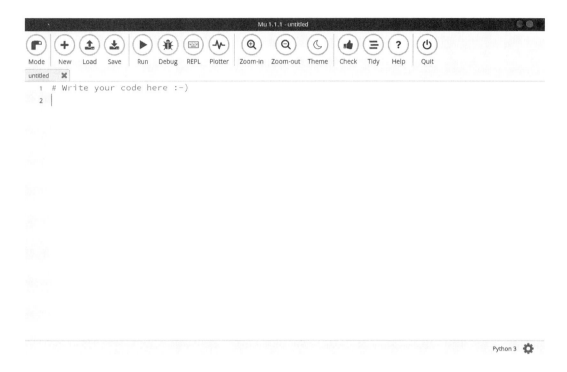

"What should I write here?" Erik asked.

"What do you want your program to do first?"

"It should say 'Welcome to Erik's Coffee Shop!'"

"Great! Let's write it. Remember the `print()` function in Python?"

Erik started to type. This first step was easy.

```
1  # Write your code here :-)
2  print("Welcome to Erik's Coffee Shop!")
3
```

Python 3

"Now what?"

"Now you run it. Click Run."

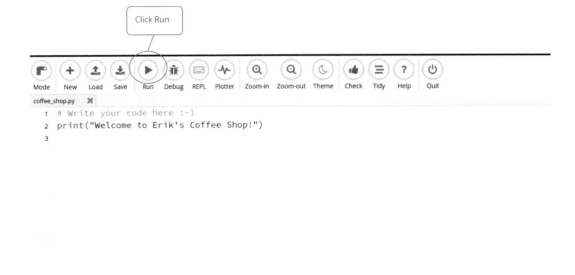

Erik clicked the button, and suddenly another window appeared asking if he wanted to save the program. That was easy. Erik typed the name of the file, `coffeeshop`, and was ready to press Enter to save the file when Simon said, "Wait, wait . . . don't forget to add `.py` to the filename. You have to let your text editor know that it's a Python program. Mu will add it automatically, but other editors won't, so make sure all your Python files are named with `.py` at the end."

Erik added `.py` to the filename and saved the file. Immediately after, he noticed another window at the bottom of the editor window. There was the coffee shop greeting—precisely as he wanted it!

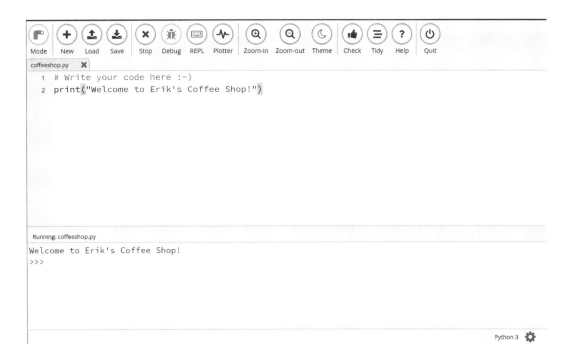

```
1  # Write your code here :-)
2  print("Welcome to Erik's Coffee Shop!")
```

Running: coffeeshop.py

```
Welcome to Erik's Coffee Shop!
>>>
```

Python 3

"It works!" Erik was delighted.

"Of course it works. Why shouldn't it?" Simon answered. "But you wanted to collect orders, didn't you?"

"Yes, I'd ask my client's name and what they want."

"And then?" Simon obviously knew the answer, but he wanted Erik to find it himself.

"And then I'd print 'Hello! Here is your order:' and show their name, flavor, and topping, like on a real receipt."

"Good idea," Simon said. "But look: when you are writing your program, you don't know what your friend wants to order, right? So you can't write in your program 'You ordered caramel.' Also, different clients order different things. It will be caramel for Alex and strawberry for Emily. So you see, your flavor *varies* from order to order, and so does the client's name. Remember what this thing is called in programming?"

"It's a *variable*!" Erik was glad he remembered that from the Python course he took several months before.

"Right!" Simon was glad too. "A variable is like a box: you can put something into it, and then open it and see what's in the box. You can also replace what's in the box with something else."

"In our case," Simon continued, "let's start with a box called answer and store whatever you hear from your client in that box. You ask your client their name, and they answer 'Alex,' for example. You put this answer in the box called answer and keep it there. When you want to print it out, you tell Python: 'Please print whatever is now in the box called `answer`.' The next client's name may be Emily, so you put 'Emily' in the box. And next time, Python will print 'Emily' not 'Alex,' because that is what is *now* in the box called `answer`. Let's write the code for this."

"Right here, in the same file?" Erik asked.

"Sure, go ahead and continue in the same file. To get something from the client, we use the *function* called `input()`. When you call it, it waits for the user to enter something. So the user types something on the keyboard and presses Enter. Then the function *returns* whatever the user entered."

"Wait, wait," Erik stopped Simon. "What do you mean—'returns'? And also, you are talking about *functions*. Of course I know what they are, but can you tell me what *you* mean by 'functions'?" Erik didn't want to show that he *barely* remembered anything about functions from his previous class.

"A function is a piece of code that *does* something. Almost every piece of code does something, but some pieces of code we use more often than others. You will create your own functions later, but for now we'll use functions written by somebody else. There are operations that people use often, such as printing something. You didn't notice it, but you already used a function when you wrote `print()` in your previous program. In programming, we say that you *call* a function."

"Aha, I see," Erik said. "Something with parentheses is called a 'function'."

"Right. And you can put something inside those parentheses, and the function will *do* something with it. For example, it will print your message. The things you pass into a function are called *arguments*. Sometimes an argument is a string, sometimes it's a number, and sometimes there are several arguments."

"What's a 'string'?" Erik asked.

"In this case, a string is a word or several words. We'll use them often, so it's good that you asked," Simon said.

"We say we '*pass arguments*' to a function," Simon continued. "The function will do something with the arguments and get something as a *result*. For example, it might calculate something, or do something with a string that you passed, like converting it to ALL CAPS or encrypting it. And then it *returns* that result to your main program."

"But how do I see the result?" Erik asked. "Will the function print it?"

"No, it won't. This is where we need *variables*. We tell Python: 'Please call this function with these arguments, and please put whatever it returns into this box, sorry, this *variable*.' All that is done using a simple 'equal' sign, like this: `=`. For example, if you want to call the `input()` function and put what it returns in the variable `answer`, you simply write this:

```
answer = input()
```

"And after you save the client's answer, you can print it. You call the `print()` function and pass your variable as an argument."

"Great," Erik said. "Now I see how to write it." He started typing in the editor. In a minute or two, he had this:

```
print("Welcome to Erik's Coffee Shop!")

answer = input()
print(answer)
```

"Should I run it?" he asked Simon.

"Sure, go ahead, click Run ⊙."

Erik clicked Run ⊙.

"It says 'Welcome to Erik's coffee shop' and then nothing."

"What did you expect?" Simon asked.

"That it would ask me my name."

"But you didn't tell Python that it should ask something. Now it's waiting for your input. Type something."

Erik typed "Erik" and pressed Enter.

Python printed `Erik`.

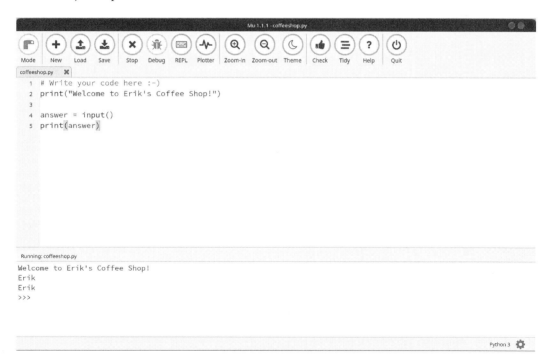

"It works!" Erik said.

Your Turn!   **Write your first dialogue**

Write the dialogue program that Erik just wrote. It's a short program, so I recommend that you type it yourself instead of copying it from the book. Create a name for your coffee shop and use it in the first "Welcome" message. Or you can create some other shop if you want. What will it sell? Ice cream? Pizza? Flowers? Pet toys?

Try to run your program. Does it do what you expect it to do? If it doesn't, copy it from the book or from the book's website (https://github.com/pavelanni/pythonicadventure-code/tree/main/ch01) and run it again. It should work.

"Yes, it works," Simon said, "but let's make it more user friendly. Remember, you were confused when it said nothing except 'Welcome.' You should tell your user what you expect from them. Also, instead of printing just Erik, you could add something like 'Here is your order, Erik.'

"You can pass this string to the input() function as an argument. We call it a *prompt* string. It explains to the user what we expect from them. And in the print() function, you can add the string you want to print before the answer variable. Let me help you."

Simon helped Erik add those strings to the code, and this is what it looked like after that:

```
print("Welcome to Erik's Coffee Shop!")

answer = input("Please enter your name: ")
print("Here is your order, ", answer)
```

Simon noticed that Erik was looking for the Run button ⊙, and he explained: "Before clicking Run ⊙ again, you have to stop your previous Python session. See the three angle brackets? They mean that Python is running and waiting for your input. I'll explain how to use Python this way later, but for now, just click Stop ⊗ and then click Run ⊙ again."

Now the program asked for the order and answered exactly as Erik programmed it:

```
Welcome to Erik's Coffee Shop!
Please enter your name: Erik
 Here is your order, Erik
>>>
```

Your Turn!   **Make your program more user friendly**

Add a prompt and an output string to your first program. Create a prompt asking the client for their name, like "Glad to see you! What's your name?"

"That looks much more user friendly, doesn't it?" Simon asked. "Always think about your users and ask yourself: 'Is it clear what I expect from the user? Can they possibly make a mistake here?'

"Now," Simon continued, "we have to ask your client about their order. You said you have coffee and chocolate. And you said something about flavors and toppings?"

"Yes," Erik said, "I want to ask them which topping and flavor they want."

"Well, go ahead and ask them. You can just repeat the same code, but don't forget to change the prompts. And I think you should print the whole order at the end, not after each question. Try it."

Erik wrote this code and stopped at the last line:

```
print("Welcome to Erik's Coffee Shop!")

answer = input("Please enter your name: ")
answer = input("Please enter your drink: ")
answer = input("Please enter your flavor: ")
answer = input("Please enter your topping: ")
print("Here is your order: ", answer)
```

"You told me to put the answers in the `answer` variable. But how do I know which is the flavor and the topping?" Erik was confused.

"Yes, I told you to put the answers in a variable, called `answer`," Simon answered. "Here we come to one of the most difficult problems in computer science: naming variables," he smiled. "Of course, you don't store all the answers in the variable called `answer`. Let's use different variables for different answers and give them meaningful names. For the client's name, we'll use a variable called `name`—that's easy. If you ask about a main drink, put the answer in the variable `drink` or `product`. For the flavor and topping answers, use the variables `flavor` and `topping`."

"At the end," Simon continued, "print each variable on a separate line, using several `print()` functions. Go ahead. I'll help you if necessary."

Erik worked on his code and finally produced this:

Listing 1.1   The first version of the coffee shop application

```
print("Welcome to Erik's Coffee Shop!")

name = input("Please enter your name: ")
drink = input("Please enter your drink: ")
flavor = input("Please enter your flavor: ")
topping = input("Please enter your topping: ")
print("Here is your order, ", name)
print("Main product: ", drink)
print("Flavor: ", flavor)
print("Topping: ", topping)
print("Thanks for your order!")
```

Erik clicked Run, and his program started a dialogue. Erik answered all the questions and got his output:

```
Welcome to Erik's Coffee Shop!
Please enter your name: Erik
Please enter your drink: coffee
```

```
Please enter your flavor: caramel
Please enter your topping: chocolate
Here is your order, Erik
Main product:  coffee
Flavor:  caramel
Topping:  chocolate
Thanks for your order!
>>>
```

Simon noticed the last line and praised Erik for his initiative: "It's always good to thank your customers."

"Yes, I saw that on several receipts in coffee shops," Erik said. He was glad he had done something on his own, besides what his older brother told him.

> ### *Your Turn!*   Add more options to the dialogue. Use variables.
> Edit your previous program and add the new lines to the dialogue. Again, feel free to change the prompts and strings you print so they're more suitable for *your* project.
>
> Change your printed output. Look at receipts from the places you visit (coffee shops, restaurants, groceries, other shops). Try to make your printed output look similar. Use text symbols like |, _, =, +, and others to make your output look interesting.

Simon decided it was time to wrap up for today.

"I think we got a good start today," he said. "Let's see what we have done so far. First, we installed your programming environment."

"Yes," Erik said. "I like this Mu editor. It uses colors to show me different parts of the program. It also shows my string in red until I put the quotes at the end. And it has a dark mode! I know that *real programmers* always use the dark mode! I think I'll keep using it."

"Second," Simon said, "we used a *function* for the first time. What was it?"

"It was the `print()` function," Erik said. "I told it what to print, and it printed it."

"Right. You *called* the function and *passed an argument* to it."

"Third," Simon continued, "you used another function to get information from the user."

"It was `input()`," said Erik. "And I saved the answers in *variables*."

"Great!" Simon was really proud of his brother. "You are making good progress."

> ### *Your Turn!*   Explain it yourself
> Try to explain it in your own words.
>
> - What is a function? Give some examples.
> - What are function arguments? Give some examples.
> - How do you call a function?
> - What is a variable? Why do you need them?
> - How should you name your variables? Why?

What is a program?

"Finally, let's add a bit more theory," Simon said. "We just built a very simple program, but it has all the main components of any other program. We asked the user for some *input*. After we received data from the user, we did something with that data. We usually call that *processing*. In our case, we just stored the data, but we could do something else with it, right?"

"For example?" Erik asked.

"For example, you've entered 'coffee' in lowercase, but we may want to start all the product and flavor names with capital letters. There is a special function in Python for that. So we can *process* the data after we receive it."

"Great idea, I want to add it!" Erik said.

"Sure, we'll do that. And finally, after we processed the data, we printed it out. In other words, we produced some *output*. Look here.

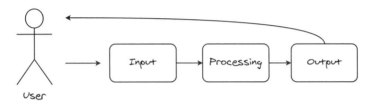

"Input doesn't always come from a user," Simon continued. "Sometimes there's no interaction with a user, and the program takes data from somewhere else. For example, from the internet, like recent sports results. Sometimes from sensors, like in robotics. Or from documents and images.

"Often, the output is not just printed. My robotics team gets inputs from sensors, we process them in the microcontroller, and our output is the signals to the motors, like 'turn left, move forward.' But the structure is still the same: input → processing → output.

"Enough theory," Simon said. "Tomorrow we'll work on improving your program."

"Improving?" Erik was surprised. "But it works fine already, doesn't it?"

"What if your user enters something you don't have in your shop?" Simon asked. "Like 'maple syrup'? What will you do? You should tell your user what you have in your coffee shop and what they can order. So tomorrow we'll work on *menus*. Also, we'll see what we can do in case of errors."

New things you have learned today

- *Variable*—A place (a box) where we can store values. For example, we can store numbers, letters, or strings. A variable can hold only one thing at a time.
- *Function*—A piece of code that does something that we want to be able to do again.
- *Function arguments*—Information that the function needs to do its job.
- *Call a function*—Write the name of the function, with parentheses and arguments between them.

Code for this chapter

You can find the code for this chapter here: https://github.com/pavelanni/ pythonicadventure-code/tree/main/ch01.

More ideas for your projects

Find more ideas for your applications at the book's companion site: https:// pythonicadventure.com/projects/. Don't worry about Flask, SQLite, and web applications (which are mentioned there) for now. We'll get to those later.

Lists:
What's on the menu?

The next day, Erik was ready to continue working on his Coffee Shop application. He remembered that Simon said something about missing products that customers might enter in the dialogue. He came to his brother and asked, "You said yesterday that customers can enter something that I don't have in the shop. What should I do about it?"

"Remember the last time you were in a coffee shop or restaurant. How did you know what you could order?"

"They had a menu with a list of products that they have in the shop."

"Right!" Simon said. "A menu! This is what we're going to create today. What does a menu look like in a coffee shop?"

"It's a list. A list of drinks like coffee, chocolate, and decaf. And a list of flavors I can add. Like caramel, mint, and others. And a list of toppings."

"Right, lists!" Simon was very glad Erik had used that word. "Like this, right?" He quickly drafted something that looked like a menu.

```
       Menu


          Drinks
Coffee          1.00
Chocolate       1.50
Decaf           1.20
       Flavors
Caramel         0.50
Vanilla         0.45
...
       Toppings
Chocolate       0.30
Cinnamon        0.30
....
```

"Lists are what we need! We have lists in Python—you may remember that. Lists are very useful in Python. They can contain numbers, strings, and even other lists. For example . . . ," Simon took another piece of paper and wrote several examples.

```
fruits = ['apple', 'peach', 'banana']

numbers = [42, 256, 1000]

constants = [3.1416, 2.718, 1.4142]
```

"Let's create lists for your menu. You just give each list a name, like `flavors`, for example, and then list your flavors in square brackets. Then do the same for your toppings and main drinks. Don't forget that your flavors, toppings, and drinks are strings, so they should be in quotes. You can start a new file in your editor and call it `menu.py`, for example."

Erik opened his editor and started typing. Here is what he had in several minutes:

```
drinks = ["chocolate", "coffee", "decaf"]
flavors = ["caramel", "vanilla", "peppermint", "raspberry", "plain"]
toppings = ["chocolate", "cinnamon", "caramel"]
```

"Very good," Simon said. "Now let's print them as menus."

"Just `print(drinks)`?" Erik suggested.

"You can do that, but it won't be pretty. Try it."

Erik added the `print()` statement at the end:

```
drinks = ["chocolate", "coffee", "decaf"]
flavors = ["caramel", "vanilla", "peppermint", "raspberry", "plain"]
toppings = ["chocolate", "cinnamon", "caramel"]
print(drinks)
```

"Click Run ▶," Simon said.

Erik clicked and saw the output at the bottom of the editor window:

```
['chocolate', 'coffee', 'decaf']
>>>
```

"If your menu is a list, we should print it as a list," Simon said. "And you should give your user a way to choose from the list. For example, you can ask them to type a letter. But here we have chocolate and coffee, so you can't just use the first letter, 'C,' for both. Let's use numbers instead. For each menu item, we'll print a number. Then your user will type the number for their choice. For example, 1 for chocolate, 2 for coffee. Something like this." Simon took a piece of paper and drew a simple menu.

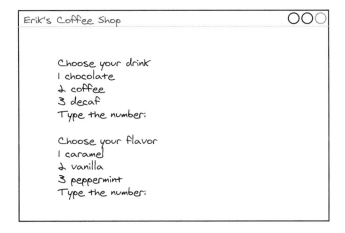

"Yes, I saw that in a Chinese restaurant—each dish had a number," Erik remembered. "But how do I do it in Python?"

"You have a list of several items," Simon started his explanation. "You have to print each item, adding a number in front of it. When we have to *repeat* something in Python, we use a *loop*. In this case it will be a `for` loop. You tell Python that for each item in the list, it has to do something. Like print it, for example.

"Write a simple `for` loop," Simon continued. "Let me write the first one for you." Simon took Erik's keyboard and added a couple of lines to his code:

```
drinks = ["chocolate", "coffee", "decaf"]
flavors = ["caramel", "vanilla", "peppermint", "raspberry", "plain"]
toppings = ["chocolate", "cinnamon", "caramel"]

for d in drinks:
    print(d)
```

Simon clicked Run, and they saw the output:

```
chocolate
coffee
decaf
>>>
```

"Now it's your turn," Simon said. "Write the same code for the other two lists. Note that I used another variable to print the list items. The list is called drinks. I used just a d for each drink in the list. It's usually best to use meaningful names for your variables, like drinks for the list of drinks. But if a variable will be used just in one loop to go through a list, the name can be short, like one or two letters. It's not a rule, but it's easier to type.

"Another important thing," Simon continued, "is that in Python, spaces mean *a lot*. You see that the print() function call is shifted four spaces to the right? This is how we tell Python *what* should be repeated in the loop. The part that is shifted right is called a *block*. Everything you put in this block will be repeated for each list item. We have only one function call in the block now, but we'll add something else later.

"You also noticed that I didn't type four spaces on the keyboard. Our editor did it for us automatically. All programming editors that you would use for Python have this feature. When they see the colon (:) they automatically shift the next line. This is called 'starting a block.' Now go ahead and write the loops."

Erik created two more loops to print the other two lists. He liked the idea of using shorter variable names (less typing!). He also noticed that the editor shifted the line after the colon automatically. Very useful! Here is what he got:

```
drinks = ["chocolate", "coffee", "decaf"]
flavors = ["caramel", "vanilla", "peppermint", "raspberry", "plain"]
toppings = ["chocolate", "cinnamon", "caramel"]

for d in drinks:
    print(d)

for f in flavors:
    print(f)

for t in toppings:
    print(t)
```

He saved the program and ran it:

```
chocolate
coffee
decaf
caramel
vanilla
peppermint
raspberry
plain
```

```
chocolate
cinnamon
caramel
>>>
```

> **Your Turn!** **Create your list of products and print it**
>
> Open your code editor and create a program similar to the one Erik just created. It should contain three or more lists of items. Then use loops to print out the content of those lists.
>
> You can use Erik's menu items or create your own. Ice cream flavors, bagels, minifigures—anything you want!

"Very good," Simon said. "But we don't have the numbers yet. We have to fix it. Remember I told you that we would add something else to the block? Here is what I propose. We'll create a variable that will keep the item's number in the list. Each time we go to the next item, we add one to that variable. In that case, 'chocolate' will be number one, 'coffee' number two, and so on.

"Let me show you," and Simon took Erik's keyboard again:

```
drinks = ["chocolate", "coffee", "decaf"]
flavors = ["caramel", "vanilla", "peppermint", "raspberry", "plain"]
toppings = ["chocolate", "cinnamon", "caramel"]

i = 1
for d in drinks:
    print(i, d)
    i = i + 1

for f in flavors:
    print(f)

for t in toppings:
    print(t)
```

He ran the program, and they saw this:

```
1 chocolate
2 coffee
3 decaf
caramel
vanilla
peppermint
raspberry
plain
chocolate
cinnamon
caramel
>>>
```

"You see: I added the `i` variable. For each list item, now I print not only its value, but also its number. And then I add one to the number to move from 1 to 2, then from 2 to 3, and so on. Now go ahead and change the rest," Simon said.

Erik made the changes:

```
drinks = ["chocolate", "coffee", "decaf"]
flavors = ["caramel", "vanilla", "peppermint", "raspberry", "plain"]
toppings = ["chocolate", "cinnamon", "caramel"]

i = 1
for d in drinks:
    print(i, d)
    i = i + 1

for f in flavors:
    print(i, f)
    i = i + 1

for t in toppings:
    print(i, t)
    i = i + 1
```

When he ran the program he saw this output:

```
1 chocolate
2 coffee
3 decaf
4 caramel
5 vanilla
6 peppermint
7 raspberry
8 plain
9 chocolate
10 cinnamon
11 caramel
>>>
```

"But this isn't what I wanted!" Erik said. "I think it should be 1, 2, 3 for the drinks, then 1, 2, 3 for the flavors, and 1, 2, 3 for the toppings again."

"Right!" Simon agreed. "How would you do this?"

"Use a different variable?"

"Yes, that's possible. But you can use the same `i` variable. The important thing is to set it to 1 before each loop. We call this *initializing* the variable."

Erik added `i = 1` before each loop and got this:

```
drinks = ["chocolate", "coffee", "decaf"]
flavors = ["caramel", "vanilla", "peppermint", "raspberry", "plain"]
toppings = ["chocolate", "cinnamon", "caramel"]

i = 1
for d in drinks:
```

```
    print(i, d)
    i = i + 1

i = 1
for f in flavors:
    print(i, f)
    i = i + 1

i = 1
for t in toppings:
    print(i, t)
    i = i + 1
```

> **Your Turn!**   **Print three (or more) menus with numbers**
>
> Modify your previous program to add numbers to your menu items. Use loops. Don't forget to reset the `i` variable (usually it's called an *item counter*) for each new list.

He clicked Run and got this output:

```
1 chocolate
2 coffee
3 decaf
1 caramel
2 vanilla
3 peppermint
4 raspberry
5 plain
1 chocolate
2 cinnamon
3 caramel
>>>
```

"Now let's make it a bit prettier," Simon said. "Add titles like 'Our drinks' before each list. Remember, we should let the user know what they are seeing and what they should do."

Erik added some titles. He even added an extra line under each title. He was sure that would make it look like a real menu:

```
drinks = ["chocolate", "coffee", "decaf"]
flavors = ["caramel", "vanilla", "peppermint", "raspberry", "plain"]
toppings = ["chocolate", "cinnamon", "caramel"]

print("Erik's Coffee Shop drinks")
print("------------------------")
i = 1
for d in drinks:
    print(i, d)
    i = i + 1

print("Erik's Coffee Shop flavors")
```

```
print("------------------------")
i = 1
for f in flavors:
    print(i, f)
    i = i + 1

print("Erik's Coffee Shop toppings")
print("------------------------")
i = 1
for t in toppings:
    print(i, t)
    i = i + 1
```

> ### *Your Turn!*   Add titles to your menus
> Add titles to your menus to make the output beautiful. Use your shop's name in the titles. Try to use other symbols, not just dashes.

The output was beautiful, as he expected:

```
Erik's Coffee Shop drinks
------------------------
1 chocolate
2 coffee
3 decaf
Erik's Coffee Shop flavors
------------------------
1 caramel
2 vanilla
3 peppermint
4 raspberry
5 plain
Erik's Coffee Shop toppings
------------------------
1 chocolate
2 cinnamon
3 caramel
>>>
```

"Looks good," Simon said. "What is also good about this format is that now you have three lists in your menu and three lists in your program.

"Now," Simon continued, "for each list in the menu, you have to ask the user to choose an item and then get that information from them. How do you get information from a user? You did it yesterday, remember?"

"With `input()`?" asked Erik.

"Of course!" Simon was glad Erik remembered the previous lesson. "You can write it yourself, can't you?"

"Let me try," Erik said and started editing his code. He remembered that he should use the `input()` function. Then he put the prompt inside the parentheses, and on the left side, he used a variable. He remembered that he shouldn't use the same variable for different questions.

Here is what he wrote:

```
drinks = ["chocolate", "coffee", "decaf"]
flavors = ["caramel", "vanilla", "peppermint", "raspberry", "plain"]
toppings = ["chocolate", "cinnamon", "caramel"]

print("Erik's Coffee Shop drinks")
print("------------------------")
i = 1
for d in drinks:
    print(i, d)
    i = i + 1
drink = input("Choose your drink: ")

print("Erik's Coffee Shop flavors")
print("-------------------------")
i = 1
for f in flavors:
    print(i, f)
    i = i + 1
flavor = input("Choose your flavor: ")

print("Erik's Coffee Shop toppings")
print("--------------------------")
i = 1
for t in toppings:
    print(i, t)
    i = i + 1
topping = input("Choose your topping: ")
```

Your Turn!   Add user inputs to your menus

Add `input()` functions to your menus. Use appropriate variable names to store the user's answers.

"Now what?" he asked Simon.

"Now your user types a number, and you use that number to find the item. In Python, we call this number a list *index*. If you put this number in square brackets next to the list name, you get that item. Like this," and he wrote an example:

drinks[drink]

"So after you know the number, you can find the item in the list. And you can print, 'Here is your order', like you did yesterday, but now you'll get those items from the menu. Try it. I'll help you if necessary."

That was a bit more difficult. Erik looked at his program from yesterday and copied the lines from it to the bottom of this program. Then he replaced variables like `drink` with the list items, like Simon suggested.

Here is his code:

```python
drinks = ["chocolate", "coffee", "decaf"]
flavors = ["caramel", "vanilla", "peppermint", "raspberry", "plain"]
toppings = ["chocolate", "cinnamon", "caramel"]

print("Erik's Coffee Shop drinks")
print("-----------------------")
i = 1
for d in drinks:
    print(i, d)
    i = i + 1
drink = input("Choose your drink: ")

print("Erik's Coffee Shop flavors")
print("-----------------------")
i = 1
for f in flavors:
    print(i, f)
    i = i + 1
flavor = input("Choose your flavor: ")

print("Erik's Coffee Shop toppings")
print("-------------------------")
i = 1
for t in toppings:
    print(i, t)
    i = i + 1
topping = input("Choose your topping: ")

print("Here is your order: ")
print("Main product: ", drinks[drink])
print("Flavor: ", flavors[flavor])
print("Topping: ", toppings[topping])
print("Thanks for your order!")
```

"Now run it, and let's see what it gives us," Simon said.

Erik clicked Run, and the program printed the drinks menu and asked for his choice. So far it worked. Erik quickly entered numbers for all three menus and saw this output:

```
Here is your order:
Traceback (most recent call last):
  File "/home/erik/mu_code/menu.py", line 30, in <module>
    print("Main product: ", drinks[drink])
TypeError: list indices must be integers or slices, not str
>>>
```

"What's this?" he was puzzled.

"Congratulations!" Simon said.

"What are you so happy about? That my program doesn't work?" Erik started getting angry at his brother.

"Not at all!" Simon said. "You got your first error message from Python, and that's a good sign! Making errors and fixing them is the only way to learn. You've got an error message—now let's try to fix the problem. Usually Python gives you the reason why this happened. Start by reading the last message. What does it say?"

"Something about slices . . . Must be integers not str. What's that?"

"I agree, it takes some practice to learn to read Python error messages. Here it tells you that when you use a variable as an index of a list, that variable should be an integer number, like 1, 2, 3."

"But I entered numbers!" Erik was still confused.

"Yes, you *typed* numbers on your keyboard. But for Python, everything you enter from a keyboard is a *string*. Python makes a difference between a string containing the number '1' and the integer number 1.

"This comes from the way computers keep things in memory," Simon continued. "The computer keeps the *number* 1 in memory, but when it shows it to you, it converts it to a *string* '1'. Computers also convert numbers they get from the keyboard. You type '123' on your keyboard, and the computer gets this string and *converts* it to a *number* 123. Look here." Simon drew a picture with a computer, keyboard, display, and a user.

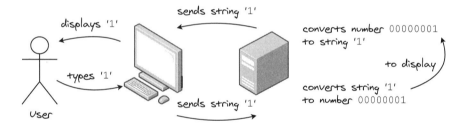

"We need to tell Python to convert the strings you type on the keyboard to integer numbers. There is a special function for that called int(). Let me show you how to use it."

Simon changed Erik's program in one place and let him do the same in the other two places. Here is what Erik's program looked like after that:

```
drinks = ["chocolate", "coffee", "decaf"]
flavors = ["caramel", "vanilla", "peppermint", "raspberry", "plain"]
toppings = ["chocolate", "cinnamon", "caramel"]

print("Erik's Coffee Shop drinks")
print("------------------------")
i = 1
for d in drinks:
    print(i, d)
    i = i + 1
drink = input("Choose your drink: ")
```

```
print("Erik's Coffee Shop flavors")
print("-------------------------")
i = 1
for f in flavors:
    print(i, f)
    i = i + 1
flavor = input("Choose your flavor: ")

print("Erik's Coffee Shop toppings")
print("-------------------------")
i = 1
for t in toppings:
    print(i, t)
    i = i + 1
topping = input("Choose your topping: ")

print("Here is your order: ")
print("Main product: ", drinks[int(drink)])
print("Flavor: ", flavors[int(flavor)])
print("Topping: ", toppings[int(topping)])
print("Thanks for your order!")
```

Converts string to a number

Erik ran the program, entered his choices (coffee, caramel, chocolate) and got this output:

```
Here is your order:
Main product:  decaf
Flavor:  vanilla
Topping:  cinnamon
Thanks for your order!
>>>
```

"What? It's all wrong!" Erik exclaimed. "This is not what I chose!"

"I didn't tell you one important thing about Python lists," Simon said. "Their indices start with zero, not one. So if you want to get the first item from the list, you should put 0 in the square brackets. If you want the second item, you use 1 as the index."

"But why?" Erik was shocked by such a strange thing.

"It's a long story," Simon answered. "It comes from the way computers store lists in memory. The index you use is the number of items you should skip from the beginning of the list to get the item you want. If you want the first item of the list, you don't have to skip any items. You just take it from the beginning of the list. So the number of items you should skip is *zero*, right? That's why the first element's index is 0. Look here." Simon drew another picture.

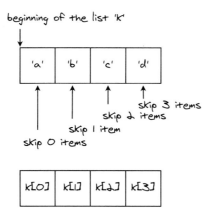

"So what should I do now?" Erik asked. He thought that he understood Simon's explanation, but he was still annoyed by this inconvenience.

"I see that you're annoyed," Simon said. "Don't worry, you'll get used to it very quickly. And you will, like all real programmers, start counting everything from zero," Simon smiled. "For now you just subtract one from each index in the square brackets. But be careful: you have to add that - 1 *after* you have converted your input to integer, not before. Like this: drinks[int(drink) - 1]."

Erik fixed his code, and now it looked like this:

```
drinks = ["chocolate", "coffee", "decaf"]
flavors = ["caramel", "vanilla", "peppermint", "raspberry", "plain"]
toppings = ["chocolate", "cinnamon", "caramel"]

print("Erik's Coffee Shop drinks")
print("-----------------------")
i = 1
for d in drinks:
    print(i, d)
    i = i + 1
drink = input("Choose your drink: ")

print("Erik's Coffee Shop flavors")
print("-------------------------")
i = 1
for f in flavors:
    print(i, f)
    i = i + 1
flavor = input("Choose your flavor: ")

print("Erik's Coffee Shop toppings")
print("-------------------------")
i = 1
for t in toppings:
    print(i, t)
    i = i + 1
topping = input("Choose your topping: ")
```

```
print("Here is your order: ")
print("Main product: ", drinks[int(drink) - 1])
print("Flavor: ", flavors[int(flavor) - 1])
print("Topping: ", toppings[int(topping) - 1])
print("Thanks for your order!")
```

Your Turn!   Modify your program to print the order

Modify your program like Erik just did and print your order. Don't forget to convert the input strings to numbers. And don't forget to subtract one (1) from each number—list indices start with zero, remember?

He ran the program, entered 2, 1, 1 and finally got what he wanted:

```
Here is your order:
Main product:  chocolate
Flavor:  caramel
Topping:  chocolate
Thanks for your order!
>>>
```

"Cool! It works!" Erik was definitely happy. "I like my coffee shop program! Are we done with it?"

"Almost," Simon answered. "Look, you wrote almost exactly the same code three times."

"What's wrong with that?"

"Imagine you want to change something in your code. For example, you may want to change the way you print the menu items. You'll have to change it in all three places. Or in even more places if you decide to add other menu lists. Imagine you want to add desserts to your coffee shop. That means you'll have to copy this code one more time. What if you made a mistake in the code? Programmers call them *bugs* (I'll tell you why later). Then you would have to fix that bug in four places, repeating yourself. Programmers like the DRY principle: *Don't Repeat Yourself.*"

"But I don't see how I can do that," Erik was confused. "If I have *three* menu lists, I have to print them three times. And I have to ask the user for input three times."

"We can use a *function* here," Simon explained. "Remember when we started using the `print()` function, I told you that for operations that we want to repeat over and over, we use functions. So far we have used functions written by somebody else. Now we'll create our own function and use it."

"That's cool. I like it," Erik said.

"Great, we'll do that tomorrow. I think we have done enough for today. You did a great job, Erik." Simon was indeed glad that his brother was making progress. "Let's recap what we have learned today. What was the first thing?"

"First, we created *lists*," Erik said. "We put all our drinks, flavors, and toppings in the lists."

"Good, what was next?"

"Then we printed the lists using *loops*. And then we printed the numbers next to each drink or flavor."

"Yes, exactly," Simon confirmed. "Go on, what was after that?"

"Then I tried to print drinks from the list, but I got an error from Python. You explained how numbers are stored in computer memory. Then we converted the numbers, and I tried to print my order again. And *just because you didn't tell me that indices start with zero*" (Erik didn't forget that!), "my order printed all the wrong items!"

"Please, forgive me," Simon smiled. "But now you'll remember it much better, I'm sure!"

"Finally I fixed it, and now it works well!" Erik finished.

"Great job!" Simon gave Erik a thumbs up. "We'll continue tomorrow and write our first function."

New things you have learned today

- *List*—A collection of items in Python. You can have strings or numbers in a list, or even a mix of them.
- *List index*—The number we use to retrieve an item from a list. Indices in lists always start with zero and increase by one for each next element: 0, 1, 2, 3, and so on.
- *Numbers and strings*—These are different *types* of variables in Python. When you print something on the screen or get input from the keyboard, you always use strings. When you want to do any math operations with numbers you received from the user, you have to convert them from strings to numbers.

Code for this chapter

You can find the code for this chapter here: https://github.com/pavelanni/pythonicadventure-code/tree/main/ch02.

Functions: Don't repeat yourself!

"Where did we stop yesterday?" Simon asked Erik the next day.

"You were going to tell me why bugs are called bugs," Erik said.

"Right!" Simon said. "Believe it or not, many years ago, computers were made of electro-mechanical things called relays that had contacts similar to light switches. One day, the engineers discovered an error in their program. Their code was correct, but they found a bug stuck between the contacts in one of the relays. That's why programmers call errors bugs. The bugs are usually hidden in your code, and you must remove them to make your program work. What else?"

34

"You said that I shouldn't repeat myself. And you said we were going to write our own function today."

"Right! First, tell me what you know about functions so far."

"We used a couple of functions already," Erik answered. "We used `print()` and `input()`. You said that somebody wrote them so we can use them. We can also use arguments with functions. We just have to put the arguments between the parentheses, and the function will do something with them, like print them."

"That's right! You're a great student!" Simon smiled. "The important thing about functions is that they can do *the same thing* each time, but with different arguments. So if you see that you're doing the same thing several times, you should look at whether it can be turned into a function. To decide, you should look at your repeating code and ask yourself which parts are the same and which are different. Where is your program from yesterday?"

"Here." Erik opened the `menu.py` file in the editor:

```
drinks = ["chocolate", "coffee", "decaf"]
flavors = ["caramel", "vanilla", "peppermint", "raspberry", "plain"]
toppings = ["chocolate", "cinnamon", "caramel"]

print("Erik's Coffee Shop drinks")
print("------------------------")
i = 1
for d in drinks:
    print(i, d)
    i = i + 1
drink = input("Choose your drink: ")

print("Erik's Coffee Shop flavors")
print("------------------------")
i = 1
for f in flavors:
    print(i, f)
    i = i + 1
flavor = input("Choose your flavor: ")

print("Erik's Coffee Shop toppings")
print("------------------------")
i = 1
for t in toppings:
    print(i, t)
    i = i + 1
topping = input("Choose your topping: ")

print("Here is your order: ")
print("Main product: ", drinks[int(drink) - 1])
print("Flavor: ", flavors[int(flavor) - 1])
print("Topping: ", toppings[int(topping) - 1])
print("Thanks for your order!")
```

"Look, what is repeating here?" Simon asked and started drawing a diagram with Erik's code.

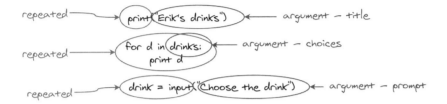

"The loop. The `print()` in the beginning and the `input()` at the end."

"And what is different in these three cases?"

"The prompt for the `input()` is different," Erik answered. "Also, the title is slightly different."

"And you're running `for` loops through different lists, like `drinks`, `flavors`, and `toppings`, right?" Simon decided to help Erik. "So we'll *pass* as arguments the things that are different. In our case, they will be the list of choices, the menu title, and the input prompt.

"Let's start a new file in the editor and call it `menu_function.py`. We'll write our function there."

Erik clicked New and then Save in the editor. He then typed `menu_function.py`, and he was ready to write code.

"Functions in Python start with the word `def` followed by the name of the function," Simon continued. "Let's call our function `menu`. Then you open the parentheses and list your arguments."

Erik wrote `def menu(` and wasn't sure what to do next.

Simon helped, "We just talked about your arguments. I see you're thinking how to name them. Remember, naming variables and arguments is one of the most difficult problems in computer science. You're not alone. Let's name them `choices`, `title`, and `prompt`. Just type them after the opening parenthesis and put a colon after the closing parenthesis."

Erik typed the following:

```
def menu(choices, title, prompt):
```

He noticed that after he pressed Enter, the cursor moved to the next line, but four spaces to the right. "Should I write here?" he asked Simon.

"Yes, sure!" Simon answered. "You see, the editor is helping you to write your function! Now look at your code from yesterday and start copying what you want to put in the function. First, we printed the title, so let's do that here too, but instead of the actual string we'll just print the *argument* called `title`. You can even put the line of dashes after it like you did before."

Erik wrote this:

```
def menu(choices, title, prompt):
    print(title)
    print("------------------------------")
```

"Now write the loop," Simon continued. "But instead of drinks or flavors, your list is now called choices. And you can use the variable c in the loop, as it's the first letter of 'choices'."

Erik copied the loop from his previous program. He added the input() function with the prompt without asking his brother:

```
def menu(choices, title, prompt):
    print(title)
    print("------------------------------")
    i = 1
    for c in choices:
        print(i, c)
        i = i + 1
    choice = input(prompt)
```

"Great!" Simon said when he saw Erik's code. "Now we have to *return* the choice."

"Can't we just print the choice variable in our main program?" Erik asked.

"No! And this is a very important thing about functions." Simon was glad that Erik had asked this question. "The variables you have inside your function are *visible* only within the function. Look here, I'll draw a picture.

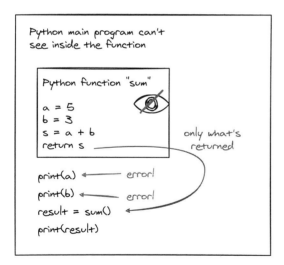

"This means that you can't see what's inside those variables when you aren't *inside the function.* So if we want our main program to see those values, we have to *return* those variables. Usually, we have many variables inside a function, but we only want to return one or two as a result. In this case, we can return the number that the user entered, which is stored in the variable `choice`."

Simon paused and thought for a moment. "But we can do better," he said. "Look at your code from yesterday again. What else is repeating?"

Erik looked and said, "Those `int()` functions, and we had to use `- 1` three times. That was annoying." He still hadn't gotten used to the fact that list indices start with zero.

"Okay, let's add them to the function too," Simon suggested. "We'll convert the user's answer to an integer, get the item from the list, and return the item, not its index. That will make our function even more useful. The main program that calls it will get the user's choice, not just some number. Let me show you," and Simon added the conversion operations and the `return` statement to the function:

```
def menu(choices, title, prompt):
    print(title)
    print("-----------------------------")
    i = 1
    for c in choices:
        print(i, c)
        i = i + 1
    choice = input(prompt)
    answer = choices[int(choice) - 1]

    return answer
```

"Now let's test it," Simon said. "In our main program that goes just below the function, we'll call it and print the answer we get. But first, we need our lists with drinks and everything. Copy them from the top of yesterday's program."

Erik added three lists just below the function. This time the lines were not shifted right and began in the first position:

```
drinks = ["chocolate", "coffee", "decaf"]
flavors = ["caramel", "vanilla", "peppermint", "raspberry", "plain"]
toppings = ["chocolate", "cinnamon", "caramel"]
```

"Good," Simon said. "Now you're ready to call your function. Pass the title, the list of drinks, and the `input` prompt. Then assign the result from the function to a variable. Call it `choice`, for example. And then print it."

Erik followed Simon's instructions, and this is what he got:

```
def menu(choices, title, prompt):
    print(title)
    print("-----------------------------")
    i = 1
    for c in choices:
        print(i, c)
        i = i + 1
    choice = input(prompt)
```

```
    answer = choices[int(choice) - 1]

    return answer

drinks = ["chocolate", "coffee", "decaf"]
flavors = ["caramel", "vanilla", "peppermint", "raspberry", "plain"]
toppings = ["chocolate", "cinnamon", "caramel"]
choice = menu(drinks, "Erik's drinks", "Choose your drink: ")
print(choice)
```

> ### *Your Turn!*   **Create your own function**
> Create your own function similar to the one Erik just created. Use your menu lists,
> titles, and prompts. Try to run it (before Erik!).

"Should I run it?" Erik asked.

"Yes, it's now ready. Go ahead!"

Erik clicked Run, and the program asked him about his drink, exactly the same
way it did before. Erik answered and got the result he expected:

```
Erik's drinks
-------------------------------
1 chocolate
2 coffee
3 decaf
Choose your drink: 2
coffee
>>>
```

"It works!" he said. "I'll add the other menus here," and he started writing. In less
than 10 minutes, he was ready to test the whole program. Now it looked like this:

```
def menu(choices, title, prompt):
    print(title)
    print("-------------------------------")
    i = 1
    for c in choices:
        print(i, c)
        i = i + 1
    choice = input(prompt)
    answer = choices[int(choice) - 1]

    return answer


drinks = ["chocolate", "coffee", "decaf"]
flavors = ["caramel", "vanilla", "peppermint", "raspberry", "plain"]
toppings = ["chocolate", "cinnamon", "caramel"]

drink = menu(drinks, "Erik's drinks", "Choose your drink: ")
flavor = menu(flavors, "Erik's flavors", "Choose your flavor: ")
topping = menu(toppings, "Erik's toppings", "Choose your topping: ")
```

```
print("Here is your order: ")
print("Main product: ", drink)
print("Flavor: ", flavor)
print("Topping: ", topping)
print("Thanks for your order!")
```

> ### *Your Turn!*   Add other menus
> Add other menus to your program. They will use the same function but with different arguments—lists of choices, titles, and prompts. Try to run it and test with *your* menu choices.

It worked as expected! Erik ran the program; entered 2, 2, 1 again; and got his order:

```
Here is your order:
Main product:  coffee
Flavor:  vanilla
Topping:  chocolate
Thanks for your order!
>>>
```

Simon said, "Notice that your program became shorter. Now if you have to change something, you only need to change it in one place."

"Why would I want to change it? It works well already," Erik said.

"Oh, there are always ways to improve your code!" Simon answered. "Let's make its title a little bit better. Did you notice that your line of dashes is now longer than the title?"

"Really? Oh, yes, you're right," Erik said. "It's because I changed the title to just 'Erik's drinks'. I can make it shorter, that's easy."

"Sure, you can make it shorter, but look—in the drinks menu, the title is shorter, and in the toppings menu, it's longer. The line of dashes should be the same length as your title string."

"But how can I do that? Maybe it's better to remove that line of dashes?" Erik was confused.

"No, I like your line here; it makes your receipt look more real. I want you to keep it. But we have to calculate the length of the title and make the line the same length. You'll learn one new function and one new operation here.

"The function we're going to use is called len(). You just put a string argument inside the parentheses, and it returns the length of the string. Let me show you. We'll use another feature of the Mu editor, called *REPL*. It stands for *Read–Eval–Print–Loop*, and it lets you use Python interactively. I usually use it when I want to test something quickly. Or to show something to somebody, like now," and Simon smiled.

"Click REPL 💻," Simon continued.

Erik clicked, and another window opened at the bottom of the Mu editor window.

"You see—you have interactive Python here," Simon said. "You can type any Python code here, and it will be executed. You can even use it as a calculator. Try typing `print('hello world')` or `2 + 2` right after `In [1]:`. In REPL, `In` means input, and the number after it is the number of your command. REPL will print `Out[1]:` and the answer. You'll see it."

```
Python3 (Jupyter) REPL

Jupyter QtConsole 4.7.7
Python 3.8.12 (default, Mar 12 2022, 19:58:23)
Type 'copyright', 'credits' or 'license' for more information
IPython 8.1.1 -- An enhanced Interactive Python. Type '?' for help.

In [1]:

                                                                    Python 3
```

Erik typed and Simon was right indeed:

```
In [1]: print('hello world')
hello world

In [2]: 2 + 2
Out[2]: 4
```

"Now let's calculate the length of a string. Type `len('abcd')`."

Erik typed and got this:

```
In [3]: len('abcd')
Out[3]: 4
```

"Now you see that the length of the string `abcd` is 4," Simon said. "You can do the same with string variables too. Use the variable `s`, put the string `'hello'` into it, and calculate its length. I'm sure you know how to do it now."

Erik typed in the REPL window and got this result:

```
In [4]: s = 'hello'

In [5]: len(s)
Out[5]: 5
```

"Good," Simon said. "Now you know that if you have a string, you can always get its length. Even more, you can get the length of a list this way. Create a list of numbers, 1, 2, 3, and get its length. Call it `n`, for example."

Erik typed:

```
In [6]: n = [1, 2, 3]

In [7]: len(n)
Out[7]: 3
```

"We'll use that later, but now let me show you one trick," Simon continued. "What will Python give me if I ask it to take a number, 2, and multiply it by 2?"

"4?" Erik wasn't sure that this was a trick. The question was too simple.

"Right. What will Python give me if I take a letter, 'A,' and multiply it by 2?"

"I don't know? 2A, maybe?"

"Go ahead and try it with interactive Python!" Simon suggested.

Erik typed and got the result:

```
In [8]: 2 * 'A'
Out[8]: 'AA'
```

"Interesting!" Erik was surprised.

"Now what if you take a dash instead of 'A' and multiply by 10?"

Erik started to guess where Simon was leading him, and he typed:

```
In [9]: 10 * '-'
Out[9]: '----------'
```

"Now replace the number 10 with the length of the string `'hello'`."

Erik got Simon's idea now:

```
In [10]: len('hello') * '-'
Out[10]: '-----'
```

> **Your Turn!**   Use REPL and experiment with the `len()` function
> Start REPL by clicking its icon in the editor. Then repeat all of Erik's experiments.
>
> Try to multiply a number by a string of two or three letters. Can you guess what the output will be?

"I see it now!" he said. "We take the `title` argument, we calculate its length, and we print a line of dashes exactly the same size!"

"Can you change your function now?" Simon asked.

"Yes, sure, I know what to do!" Erik had started typing already. He changed only the third line, and now his function looked like this:

```
def menu(choices, title, prompt):
    print(title)
    print(len(title) * '-')        ⟵  Repeats the dash (-)
    i = 1                              multiple times
    for c in choices:
        print(i, c)
        i = i + 1

    choice = input(prompt)
    answer = choices[int(choice) - 1]

    return answer
```

> ### *Your Turn!*   Change your function to print the correct line of dashes
> Make a change in your program to print the correct number of dashes, similar to what Erik just did. Try using a different symbol—an equal sign (=), or underscore (_), or something else.

Erik tested the main program, and now all the lines of dashes were exactly the same size as their titles.

Simon commented, "Now you see that not only is the result your function returns dependent on the arguments, but what it prints can be dependent as well.

"It's always a good idea to analyze the arguments you receive in your function," Simon continued. "In this case, we checked the title's length. What would your function do if it received an empty string with length zero?"

"I don't know," Erik answered. "I think it would print an empty string—nothing."

"Right," Simon said. "But maybe we can still print something reasonable, even if the title is empty. Maybe just 'Erik's Menu' and a line of dashes. For such cases in Python, we have *default* values for function arguments. In your function, I'd change the first line to this." Simon edited Erik's file:

```
def menu(choices, title="Erik's Menu", prompt="Choose your item: "):
```

"In this case, we tell Python, 'If there *is* a `title` argument, then accept its value.' If you didn't pass a `title` when you called your function, the function will use its default value, which is `Erik's Menu`. It's usually recommended that you set default values. You can always change them to something else when you call your function.

"Let's test it," Simon suggested. "In your first call with `drinks`, remove both the title and the prompt. Leave only `drinks` as a single argument."

Erik did what Simon suggested, and the first function call looked like this:

```
drink = menu(drinks)
```

He ran the program again and saw the first menu:

```
Erik's Menu
-----------
1 chocolate
2 coffee
3 decaf
Choose your item:
```

Here is Erik's full program.

Listing 3.1   The full menu program with a function

```
def menu(choices, title="Erik's Menu", prompt="Choose your item: "):
    print(title)
```

```
    print(len(title) * "-")
    i = 1
    for c in choices:
        print(i, c)
        i = i + 1
    choice = input(prompt)
    answer = choices[int(choice) - 1]

    return answer


drinks = ["chocolate", "coffee", "decaf"]
flavors = ["caramel", "vanilla", "peppermint", "raspberry", "plain"]
toppings = ["chocolate", "cinnamon", "caramel"]

drink = menu(drinks)
flavor = menu(flavors, "Erik's flavors", "Choose your flavor: ")
topping = menu(toppings, "Erik's toppings", "Choose your topping: ")

print("Here is your order: ")
print("Main product: ", drink)
print("Flavor: ", flavor)
print("Topping: ", topping)
print("Thanks for your order!")
```

Your Turn!   Use default arguments in your function

Add default values for your `title` and `prompt` arguments. Try to call your function without those arguments and make sure it uses the default values.

"Of course, now it's not telling the user that it's a *drinks* menu, but it's still better than an empty string. This is helpful when you want to test something quickly. You can always add more descriptive titles and prompts later.

"I think that's enough for today," Simon said. "Let's recap what you have learned. What was the first thing today?"

"We looked at the program I wrote yesterday and found things that were repeated three times. And you told me that we could write our own function. You told me about the word def and the arguments."

"Good, go ahead," Simon encouraged Erik. "What about those arguments?"

"I used the list of choices, the title, and the prompt as arguments in my function." Erik liked to talk about *his* function—he wrote it himself for the first time!

"Then you showed me that *REPL* thing in the editor," Erik continued. "I like it! And then we calculated the string's length."

"And what did we use it for?" Simon asked.

"We used it to print our receipts, and now they look beautiful. And then we tried to use default values for arguments. It was a bit boring, but it worked."

Simon said, "This is a very important thing that you just said. Good programming solutions often look boring, but they work. Programming is not always about fancy tricks and hacks. Most of the time you have to do very boring things, like check a user's input, check for errors, and so on. But if doing this boring stuff makes your program work, it's worth it. Tomorrow we'll see what you have to do to make sure your program works even if your user enters wrong values. But for now—get some rest! You did a great job today!"

New things you have learned today

- *Function*—A piece of programming code that can be used (called) repeatedly. A function can be written by you or somebody else. If it's written by somebody else, it's usually part of a *library* or a *module* in Python.
- *Arguments*—Variables that we pass to a function when we call it. The function takes the arguments and uses them to prepare its output. The output can be printed or *returned* to the main program.
- *REPL*—Read–Eval–Print–Loop, a way to run Python interactively. It's very useful for testing functions quickly.

Code for this chapter

You can find the code for this chapter here: https://github.com/pavelanni/pythonicadventure-code/tree/main/ch03.

User errors: Everybody makes mistakes

In this chapter

- Erik discovers that users don't always do what you tell them to
- Erik learns how to use loops to repeat his question to the user
- Simon helps Erik make the menus more robust

"Yesterday you did a great job, Erik," Simon said the next day. "You wrote a very good function, you added default arguments, and you tested it."

"Yes," Erik answered. "I think it's a good program. I want to show it to my friends!"

"Wait, wait," Simon said. "I don't think it's ready to use yet."

"Why? I think it works perfectly!"

"Oh, really? Let me try." Simon looked like he had something in mind. He started Erik's program again, and at the first menu he entered coffee:

```
Erik's drinks
--------------------------------
1 chocolate
2 coffee
3 decaf
Choose your drink: coffee
 Traceback (most recent call last):
  File "/home/erik/mu_code/menu_function.py", line 18, in <module>
    drink = menu("Erik's drinks", drinks, "Choose your drink: ")
  File "/home/erik/mu_code/menu_function.py", line 9, in menu
    answer = choices[int(choice) - 1]
ValueError: invalid literal for int() with base 10: 'coffee'
>>>
```

Error messages from Python

"What are you doing?" Erik was enraged. "You should enter only numbers and not words!"

"But you gave me a list and asked what I wanted. I wanted coffee, so I entered coffee. What's wrong?" Simon tried to look innocent, but he couldn't hide his smile.

"Well, for such *stupid* users like you, I'll print in ALL CAPS that you should enter a *number*!" Erik grumbled.

"Okay, okay, let me try again," said Simon. He started the program again, and at the first menu, he entered 42:

```
Choose your drink: 42
 Traceback (most recent call last):
  File "/home/erik/mu_code/menu_function.py", line 18, in <module>
    drink = menu("Erik's drinks", drinks, "Choose your drink: ")
  File "/home/erik/mu_code/menu_function.py", line 9, in menu
    answer = choices[int(choice) - 1]
IndexError: list index out of range
>>>
```

Error messages from Python

"Again? You broke it again?" Erik was ready to slap Simon's hands on the keyboard. "Didn't you see that there are only three choices? Why did you enter 42?"

"First, because 42 is my favorite number. Second, yes, it was my mistake. Users make mistakes, you know. Seriously, I wanted to show you that your program should be ready for that. You can print whatever you want, in all caps, but there *will* be users who won't read it. There *will* be users who make mistakes."

"What should I do about it?" Erik was still angry at his brother, but he tended to agree with him. He made mistakes with programs himself.

"You should check what the user enters and tell them if the input is wrong. Let's think what we can do here.

"What should the user enter in the first menu?" Simon asked.

"They should enter 1, 2, or 3," Erik answered.

"Okay, so we can check if their answer was 1, or 2, or 3, and then we pass it to the function and pick that item from the list of options. But if it's not, we should tell the user that something is wrong."

"Yes, I remember. We can use `if-else` in Python," Erik suggested.

"Let's try it," Simon said. "How will you do that? Try to explain it to me as if I didn't know about `if-else`."

"I'll add to my function, 'if the user's choice is 1, or 2, or 3, then go ahead and use it. If not (`else`), print that the user should enter one of those numbers'."

"And how do you check if the user's choice is 1, or 2, or 3? How do we do it in Python?" Simon asked.

"I don't remember . . . ," Erik said.

"You need to use a *comparison* operator. It uses two equal signs, like this: `==`. For example, to check if `choice` is equal to 1, you'd write `choice == '1'`."

"But I want to check all three numbers," Erik said. "Should I write `if choice == '1' or '2' or '3'`?"

"You're almost right!" Simon answered. "Yes, you can use `or` in Python, but in this case, you should write it as three *separate* comparisons and place `or` between them. Like this," and he wrote this code on a piece of paper:

```
if choice == '1' or choice == '2' or choice == '3':
```

"Okay, got it," Erik said.

"Good, let's code it," Simon said.

Erik opened his editor and added the four lines before `return` to his function:

```
def menu(choices, title="Erik's Menu", prompt="Choose your item: "):
    print(title)
    print(len(title) * "-")
    i = 1
    for c in choices:
        print(i, c)
        i = i + 1
    choice = input(prompt)

    if choice == '1' or choice == '2' or choice == '3':
        answer = choices[int(choice) - 1]
    else:
        print("Enter number 1, 2, or 3!")

    return answer
```

"Now let's try it," Simon said.

Erik started the program, and at the first menu, he typed 2.

"Why did you enter 2?" Simon asked.

"Because I wanted coffee," Erik answered.

"But we should test your program for *wrong* answers!" Simon said. "Yes, I know, it's your program and you don't want to break it, but as a developer you *have* to try to break your program. You have to imagine all the possible wrong ways your users will use your program. It's hard and very uncomfortable, I know, but you have to overcome that and try to enter all the possible wrong values."

"Okay, okay," Erik said and restarted his program. At the first menu, he entered 42 like Simon did the last time (Erik's input is shown in bold.):

```
Erik's Menu
-----------
1 chocolate
2 coffee
3 decaf
Choose your item: 42                          Python shows you where the error is.
 Enter number 1, 2, or 3!
Traceback (most recent call last):
  File "/home/erik/mu_code/menu_function.py", line 21, in <module>
    drink = menu(drinks)
  File "/home/erik/mu_code/menu_function.py", line 14, in menu
    return answer
UnboundLocalError: local variable 'answer' referenced before assignment   <-
>>>                                           Python tells you what the error is.
```

NOTE You can learn more about Python error messages at the book's companion site: https://pythonicadventure.com/troubleshooting/index.html.

"Let's see what's going on here," Simon said. "First of all, when you entered 42, your program printed the message that the user should enter only 1, 2, or 3. This is good. But then something went wrong. Look, it says that the variable answer was referenced before assignment:

```
UnboundLocalError: local variable 'answer' referenced before assignment
```

"In simple words, that means you didn't create answer but you tried to use it. And Python shows you exactly where: you tried to return answer, but Python didn't know anything about the variable answer."

"But why?" Erik said. "I have this answer = line in my code."

"Yes, you have it, but the important thing is *where* this line is used. In your code, you create the answer variable *only* when the user enters the right choice. If the user enters something else, answer is not even created.

"In other words," Simon continued, "even when the user answers with a wrong number, or even a word, you still have to return *some* answer. It's a very important rule: never use a variable before you create it and assign *some* value to it. What value can we assign to answer here in case the user makes a mistake? An empty string like ' ' should work here. Add it to your function and check if it helps."

Erik changed the function to this:

```
def menu(choices, title="Erik's Menu", prompt="Choose your item: "):
    print(title)
    print(len(title) * "-")
    i = 1
    for c in choices:
        print(i, c)
```

```
        i = i + 1
  choice = input(prompt)

  if choice == '1' or choice == '2' or choice == '3':
      answer = choices[int(choice) - 1]
  else:
      print("Enter number 1, 2, or 3!")        An empty line
      answer = ''                          ◄──  assigned to answer.

  return answer
```

> ### *Your Turn!*   Add code to check the user's answer
> In your menu function, add the code that Erik just added. Make sure you assign an empty line to `answer` in case the input is wrong. Test whether it really checks your answers.

He tested the program again, and this time it didn't give him an error. It printed the message `Enter number 1, 2, or 3!` and jumped to the next menu.

"Do you think your program did it right?" Simon asked.

"It printed the message that you should enter 1, 2, or 3," Erik answered. "I think it's right."

"But you didn't get the user's choice for a drink. If they entered a wrong number, you should give them a chance to enter a right one. It's not like a test in school, where you just have one chance to answer. You should keep asking the user until you get one of the right answers."

"How should I do that?" Erik asked.

"There is another kind of *loop* for that," Simon explained to his brother. "It's called a *while loop*. It repeats something over and over again, and with every cycle, it checks the *condition*. When the condition is true, it continues. If it becomes false, the loop ends.

"Sometimes we check the condition at the beginning of the loop if we already know it. In this case, we say 'While something is true, do this.' But sometimes, like in our case, we don't have the answer when we start the loop, because we haven't asked our user about their choice yet. So we start an *infinite loop* and check the condition *inside* the loop—after we receive an answer from the user. We exit the loop if the condition becomes true. We call this *breaking* from the loop. Let me show it in a sketch," Simon said and started drawing.

Simon explained, "In this example, we already know the condition before we start the loop. We check the condition and decide if we should start. It should be `True`, or the loop won't even start. I used a *diamond-shaped* figure for this check; this is how programmers usually draw decision points.

"If it's true, then we do something. The important thing is that this 'do something' should change the condition, among other things. Otherwise, the loop will continue forever, and we don't want that.

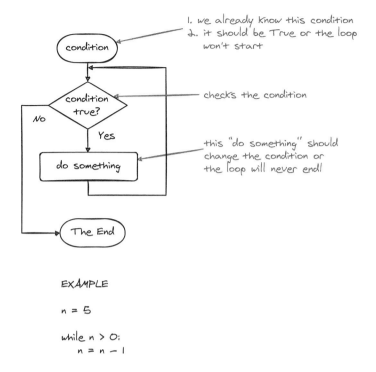

1. we already know this condition
2. it should be True or the loop won't start

condition

checks the condition

condition true?

No

Yes

this "do something" should change the condition or the loop will never end!

do something

The End

EXAMPLE

n = 5

while n > 0:
    n = n − 1

"After we have done that 'something,' we go to the beginning of the loop and *check the condition again.* If it's still true, we repeat that 'do something.' If not, we exit the loop and continue with our program.

"Look at this simple example: we want to count down from 5 to 0. First, we set the variable n to 5, and at the beginning of the loop, we check if it's greater than 0. Yes, it's greater, so we start the loop. Remember that we have to change the condition at some point, or the loop will never end. In our example, we subtract 1 from n each time we go through the loop. Eventually, the variable n will become equal to 0, and the loop will stop.

"The important thing is that, in this case, before we start the loop, we already know what is in the variable n, and we know that it's greater than 0.

"What if we don't know what's in the variable, or if the variable doesn't even exist? Like in our case, we can check the user's answer only *after* we ask them to choose one of the items from the menu. So we have to do this," and Simon drew another diagram.

Simon continued his explanation, "Here, we start the loop without checking any condition. We do something first, and only *after that* do we check the condition. Sometimes this loop is called 'do-until,' which means 'do something until the condition is true.' When the condition is true, we exit the loop and continue with the rest of the program.

In the example here, I used your situation with input(). You ask for input, and then you check that input. This is your condition: if the input is valid, you should exit the loop. In Python, we use the break operator for that."

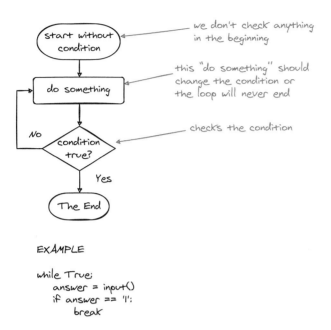

we don't check anything
in the beginning

this "do something" should
change the condition or
the loop will never end

checks the condition

EXAMPLE

```
while True:
    answer = input()
    if answer == '1':
        break
```

Erik was a bit overwhelmed by this long explanation, but he felt like he knew what to do. He asked his brother, "So you're saying that I should just put a while in front of my input() line and add a break after I get a correct answer?"

"Yes," Simon answered, "exactly right! Just don't forget to indent all the lines that are part of the loop by four spaces to the right. Your editor will help you, don't worry."

Erik started working on his program. After several minutes, his function looked like this:

```
def menu(choices, title="Erik's Menu", prompt="Choose your item: "):
    print(title)
    print(len(title) * "-")
    i = 1
    for c in choices:
        print(i, c)
        i = i + 1
    while True:
    choice = input(prompt)
    if choice == '1' or choice == '2' or choice == '3':
        answer = choices[int(choice) - 1]
        break
    else:
        print("Enter number 1, 2, or 3!")
        answer = ''

    return answer
```

"Right?" Erik asked his brother.

"I told you that your editor can help you. Click Check 👍."

Erik did as his brother suggested and saw this:

```
def menu(choices, title="Erik's Menu", prompt="Choose your item: "):
    print(title)
    print(len(title) * "-")
    i = 1
    for c in choices:
        print(i, c)
        i += 1
    while True:
    choice = input(prompt)
    ↑ Syntax error. Python cannot understand this line. Check for missing characters!
    ↑ Expected an indented block
    if choice == '1' or choice == '2' or choice == '3':
        answer = choices[int(choice) - 1]
        break
    else:
        print("Enter number 1, 2, or 3!")
        answer = ''

    return answer
```

"You see now?" Simon said. "You forgot to indent the lines to the right. That's why it says that it expects an indented block here. Move all the lines that are part of the loop to the right."

Erik changed his function and checked the code again:

```
def menu(choices, title="Erik's Menu", prompt="Choose your item: "):
    print(title)
    print(len(title) * "-")
    i = 1
    for c in choices:
        print(i, c)
        i = i + 1
    while True:              ◁——— While loop begins here.
        choice = input(prompt)
        if choice == '1' or choice == '2' or choice == '3':   If the answer is
            answer = choices[int(choice) - 1]                 right, exit from
            break                            ◁————————         the loop.
        else:
            print("Enter number 1, 2, or 3!")
            answer = ''                End of the indented
                                ◁———— block; end of the loop

    return answer
```

Your Turn! Add a `while` loop to your function

Add a loop like Erik just did. Try using the Check button to find out if there are errors in your code. Make some errors and see if the editor can find them.

Now the Check button showed a green thumbs-up 👍 for a moment, so Erik knew it was okay. He clicked Run to test the program. At the first menu, he entered 42 like Simon did last time. The program reported that he should choose 1, 2, or 3 and returned to the prompt again. It didn't crash; it worked!

"What was the other wrong thing Simon did with my program?" Erik tried to remember. "Right, he tried to enter 'coffee'! Let's try that too."

He entered coffee, and his program responded as he expected again! Finally, Erik typed 2 and got the next menu. Here is what he saw in the editor window:

```
Erik's Menu
-----------
1 chocolate
2 coffee
3 decaf
Choose your item: 42
 Enter number 1, 2, or 3!
Choose your item: coffee
 Enter number 1, 2, or 3!
Choose your item: 2
 Erik's flavors
 --------------
```

At the next menu, he typed 4 for raspberry and got the same message:

```
Erik's flavors
--------------
1 caramel
2 vanilla
3 peppermint
4 raspberry
5 plain
Choose your flavor: 4
 Enter number 1, 2, or 3!
Choose your flavor:
```

"Why is that?" he asked Simon.

"Your program behaves exactly as you wrote it," Simon answered. Of course, he knew where the problem was.

"How did you write your condition?" he asked.

Erik said, "If the answer is 1, 2, or 3—aha, I understand now! I entered 4, so the program thinks it's a wrong answer! But how can I fix this?"

"It looks like we need a list of valid answers for each menu list," Simon said. "You can pass it as another argument. But I think you know enough already to create a better solution."

"What is it?" Erik asked. "Something with loops again?"

"Not only loops," Simon answered. "You'll learn something new about lists, too. Yes, I know that you are tired of my lectures, but let's finish it today. It will make your program work correctly again—isn't that worth it?" and he winked at his brother.

Erik was tired, but that bug (yes, he had learned that word!) with the flavors menu was really annoying, and he wanted to fix it. "Okay," he sighed, "let's fix it. What did you want to tell me about lists?"

"Look at your condition," Simon said. "You used a simple `if-else` check, and you checked the input against three valid answers: 1, 2, and 3. But what if your list of items is long, like 20 items? Your `if-else` block would be too long. There is another way in Python. We can check if a certain item is in a list. In our case, we can check if the answer we got from the user is in the list of 1, 2, 3. We can try that for the first menu. Let me show you."

Simon took Erik's keyboard and changed the `if choice == . . .` line in his function to the following:

```
. . .
    while True:
        choice = input(prompt)
        if choice not in ['1', '2', '3']:
            answer = choices[int(choice) - 1]
            break
        else:
            print("Enter number 1, 2, or 3!")
            answer = ''
. . .
```

"This needs some explanation," he said. "Look, the user enters a string that can be 1 or 42. We test whether this string is in the list of allowed answers, which is 1, 2, or 3. If it's not in the list, we print the error message and continue with the loop. If it *is* in the list of allowed answers, we convert it and pick that item from the menu list."

"Yes, I understand," Erik said. "But what about the second menu where I got the error? It didn't let me choose number 4 because it wasn't in my `if`. With your list, I'll have the same problem. I have five flavors, so I need another list of answers here, right?"

"Excellent question!" Simon said. "I was just about to ask it myself. And you are right. Each menu list should have its own list of allowed answers. That's not a big problem; we can build one when we know what's in our menu list. Let me write it first, and then I'll explain it step by step." Simon added the following lines just before the `if` block he added previously:

```
. . .
    while True:
        choice = input(prompt)
        allowed_answers = []          ← An empty list for
        for a in range(1, len(choices)+1):   allowed answers
            allowed_answers.append(str(a))    ← Calculates the
        if choice not in allowed_answers:      length of the menu
            answer = choices[int(choice) - 1]
            break                             ← Appends the
        else:                                  allowed answer
            print("Enter number 1, 2, or 3!")
            answer = ''
. . .
```

"First, we create an empty list for the allowed answers. Then we measure the length of the menu list using the `len()` function. For your drinks, the result will be three, and for the flavors, it will be five. Then we use the `range()` function to create a *sequence* of numbers from one to the length of the menu. For drinks, the sequence will be 1, 2, 3. For flavors, it will be 1, 2, 3, 4, 5. You get the idea. Just notice that in the `range()` function, we shouldn't use the *last* element of the sequence, but the one *after the last*, which is not included in the sequence. That's why we have to add one to the length of the menu, like this:

```
len(choices)+1
```

"Finally, in the `for` loop, we convert each number from the sequence to a string and add it to the end of the list of allowed answers. This function is called `append()`."

Simon finished his explanation and added, "Yes, it's a bit complicated the first time, but try reading the Python code yourself, and you'll understand it as if it were plain English.

"Now we have to change our list with 1, 2, 3 to the list of allowed answers that we just built." Simon made that change, looked at the code, and slapped his forehead. "Oh, I just noticed!"

"What?" Erik thought they had already finished, but it looked like there was something else.

"We also have to change our message," Simon said. "Because our function now can accept menu lists of any length, we should tell the user something like, 'Enter a number from 1 to 6' or 'from 1 to 12,' depending on the length of our menu. Remember how we can get the length of a list?"

"With the `len()` function?" asked Erik.

"Of course!" Simon said and made the final change in the function. It now looked like this:

```
def menu(choices, title="Erik's Menu", prompt="Choose your item: "):
    print(title)
    print(len(title) * "-")
    i = 1
    for c in choices:
        print(i, c)
        i = i + 1
    while True:
        choice = input(prompt)
        allowed_answers = []
        for a in range(1, len(choices)+1):
            allowed_answers.append(str(a))

        if choice in allowed_answers:
            answer = choices[int(choice) - 1]
            break
        else:
            print("Enter number from 1 to ", len(choices))    ◁──┐ len() is used to
            answer = ''                                              calculate the
                                                                     number of
    return answer                                                    choices.
```

> **Your Turn!** **Add the** `allowed_answers` **list**
>
> Add a list of allowed answers to your function. Test whether it allows you to use menu lists of different lengths.

"Now we're protected from user errors!" Simon said. "Try it and see if it works!"

Erik ran the program again and entered `42`, `coffee`, and `weryiuryt587456`, but the program didn't crash like before. Every time, it gave him a reminder that he should use a number, and it should be between 1 and 3 or 5, depending on the menu.

"This is cool! It works and it doesn't crash!" Erik was really happy that he had created such a robust program.

"One more thing," Simon said. "This one will be the final one for today, I promise!"

"Okay," said Erik. He was starting to like this programming thing. He liked that his program now looked like a real one—and it worked! Even if it wasn't an online or mobile application yet, it worked like a chat with a shop. Erik imagined that he was texting with his favorite coffee shop, ordering his drinks, and then coming to pick them up.

Simon said, "Your program doesn't let me enter anything except the numbers from 1 to 3 or 5. But what if I want to skip something? Like I don't want any toppings on my drink?"

"In my flavors menu, I have 'plain,' which means 'no flavor.' I can add the same to toppings," Erik answered.

"That will work," Simon said. "But in general, with every menu you should give your user an option to exit the menu. Usually, people use something like 'Click X to exit from this menu.' I think we should add this to our menu function too."

"How do we do it?" Erik asked. He thought a little and said, "I know! We'll add 'X' to the list of allowed answers! Am I right?"

"Absolutely!" Simon was very glad to see his brother making such good progress. "Remember, we used the function called `append()` to add items to the list? We can use it here, right after we finish adding numbers to allowed_answers."

"Let me try," Erik said and started typing.

"Sure, go ahead," Simon encouraged his brother. "Just make sure you add it *after* that `for` loop. Better to add an empty line after it; that way you'll be able to see that it's not part of the loop."

Here is Erik's new version of the menu function:

```
def menu(choices, title="Erik's Menu", prompt="Choose your item: "):
    print(title)
    print(len(title) * "-")
    i = 1
    for c in choices:
        print(i, c)
        i = i + 1
    while True:
        choice = input(prompt)
```

```
    allowed_answers = []
    for a in range(1, len(choices)+1):
        allowed_answers.append(str(a))

    allowed_answers.append('X')        ⟵── 'X' is now an allowed answer.

    if choice in allowed_answers:
        answer = choices[int(choice) - 1]
        break
    else:
        print("Enter number from 1 to ", len(choices))
        answer = ''

return answer
```

"Nice," Simon said. "I would also add the lowercase letter 'x', because that's what most people would type. Now what should we do if the user types 'x'?"

"Exit the menu loop?" Erik said.

"Right! But what are we going to return to the main program? Normally, we return the user's choice from the menu: coffee or chocolate or whatever. What if the user types 'x'? What should we return?"

"Nothing?" Erik suggested.

"Yes, we return an empty string," Simon said. "If the user types 'x', you assign an empty string (`''`) to `answer` and return `answer` the same way you do when the answer is in the menu."

Simon continued, "Important thing: you should do that check *before* you try to convert it into a number but *after* you check whether it's in the `allowed_answers` list. Do you see where to put this check?"

"Yes, right after this line: `if choice in allowed_answers`."

"Great! Go ahead and add it. In this case, you will have a *nested* `if` statement—one `if` inside another `if`. This is pretty common—sometimes you see three levels of nested `if`s or even more. Just make sure your indentations are correct. This is how Python tells the computer what to do if the condition is true or false."

Erik worked some more on his code and finally got this:

Listing 4.1   The final version of Erik's menu

```
def menu(choices, title="Erik's Menu", prompt="Choose your item: "):
    print(title)
    print(len(title) * "-")
    i = 1
    for c in choices:
        print(i, c)
        i = i + 1
    while True:
        choice = input(prompt)
        allowed_answers = []
        for a in range(1, len(choices)+1):
            allowed_answers.append(str(a))
```

```
        allowed_answers.append('X')
        allowed_answers.append('x')

        if choice in allowed_answers:
            if choice == 'X' or choice == 'x':
                answer = ''
                break
            else:
                answer = choices[int(choice) - 1]
                break
        else:
            print("Enter number from 1 to ", len(choices))
            answer = ''

    return answer
```

> ### *Your Turn!* Add the exit option
> Add the `'x'` option to your lists of allowed answers. Then add a nested `if` to check it.
> Test whether it works. What if you enter `'x'` in all the menus? What order will you get
> in that case?

He tested the program, entering x in all three menus, and he got what he expected:

```
Erik's Menu
-----------
1 chocolate
2 coffee
3 decaf
Choose your item: x
Erik's flavors
--------------
1 caramel
2 vanilla
3 peppermint
4 raspberry
5 plain
Choose your flavor: x
Erik's toppings
---------------
1 chocolate
2 cinnamon
3 caramel
Choose your topping: x
Here is your order:
Main product:
Flavor:
Topping:
Thanks for your order!
```

"An empty order!" he said.

"Right, exactly as it should be," Simon confirmed. "I like your program," he continued. "It works—that's the first and most important part. It's user friendly, and it gives the user instructions on what to do—that's the second part. It checks the input and it doesn't let the user enter wrong values—that's the third part.

"Let's quickly recap what you learned today," Simon said. "What was the first thing?"

"First you broke my program, again!" Erik answered. He wasn't very angry this time, because he knew that together with Simon he had fixed the program. "And you told me that I should always think about how my users might use the program in a bad way."

"Right, dealing with stubborn users who don't want to follow your instructions is part of a programmer's job," Simon said.

"Then we wrote a menu loop where we checked what the user entered, and we didn't allow them to use answers that aren't allowed. Then you told me about the `append()` function that adds something to a list."

Erik continued, "Then I wrote *nested* `if` checks, and now my code looks like real programs they show in movies."

Simon smiled, "Trust me, programs they show in movies are very rarely real programs. But you're right, your program is getting more complex. It uses different Python operators, all these loops, and `if`s, and lists."

"And then we added the 'x' option in the menu, and now any user can get an empty order!" Erik giggled.

"Yes, and why not?" Simon asked. "You shouldn't *force* your users to always order something. You should give them an option to cancel their order or to exit from the menu."

Simon continued, "The program is really good now. Tomorrow I'll ask you to stop being a programmer and become the coffee shop manager."

"Am I not a manager already?" Erik asked.

"Yes, you are," Simon smiled. "Now imagine that you, the coffee shop manager, just received a new flavor component for your coffee drinks. And you want to add that flavor to the menu. And a couple of new toppings. What would you do?"

"I would add those toppings to the list of toppings. Not a big deal," Erik answered.

"Yes, but what if you are *just* a manager and not a programmer? You know nothing about this program, and you don't know Python, but you want to add those flavors and toppings to the menu. You, as a programmer, should give the manager an easy way to add something to the menu."

"How do you suggest I do that?" Erik asked. He knew already that Simon had something in mind.

"I think we should put the menus in files and read your lists from those files."

"Like in Word documents?" Erik asked.

"Yes, almost," Simon said. "Your program will open those files and read from them. I think it will be easiest to have one file per menu. One file will have all the drinks, another one all the flavors, and another all the toppings. Then your manager can just edit those files instead of editing your Python code. Sound good?"

"Yes, interesting," Erik said. He wondered how his Python program would open files the same way Word does.

"Great," Simon said. "That is what we're going to do tomorrow. Take a rest now."

New things you have learned today

- *Users make mistakes*—You have learned that users don't always follow the directions you give them in your program. You have to be ready for that and check their input for errors, wrong types, and so on.
- *Indentation*—When you create a *block* in Python (like `while`, for example) you have to make sure all the code in the block is *indented*, meaning it's shifted to the right.
- *How to exit from a menu*—You have to give your users a way to exit from each menu. For example, if they don't want to order a topping, they may want to skip that menu.

Code for this chapter

You can find the code for this chapter here: https://github.com/pavelanni/ pythonicadventure-code/tree/main/ch04.

5

Working with files: Being a shop manager

"Last time, you said something about a coffee shop manager," Erik started with his brother the next day. "Something about changing menus? I forgot."

"Yes, I said it might be good if your coffee shop manager could change the menus without going into Python code," Simon said.

"Yes, good idea," Erik said. "Not everyone knows Python."

"My idea is to create simple text files for each menu—call them `drinks.txt`, `flavors.txt`, and `toppings.txt`. Then your program can read from those files and create lists from the items in the files."

"Why did you name them all with `.txt` at the end?" Erik asked. "Shouldn't they be `.docx` so the manager could edit them in Microsoft Word?"

"Good point," Simon said. "Yes, the manager might be more familiar with Word, but we need a *plain text file*, without fonts, headers, or a table of contents. It's similar to your Python code—these files should have nothing but lines of plain text, and the manager should use a plain text editor to work with them. When I name them with .txt at the end, I tell the operating system—whether it's Windows, macOS, or Linux—that this file should be opened with a plain text editor and not a word processor like Word. In all those systems, there is always a text editor that can edit these files. You can also install another application for that, like we did with the Mu editor. Also, it's much easier for Python to read from a plain text file than from a .docx file.

"Let's create these files," Simon continued. "You can use your Mu editor for that. Just don't forget to add the .txt extension when saving the files. Otherwise, it will automatically add .py.

"Create a new file, enter your drinks on separate lines, and save it with the name drinks.txt. Then do the same for flavors and toppings."

Erik started working. After several minutes he had three files:

Listing 5.1 drinks.txt

```
coffee
chocolate
decaf
```

Listing 5.2 flavors.txt

```
caramel
vanilla
peppermint
raspberry
plain
```

Listing 5.3 toppings.txt

```
chocolate
cinnamon
caramel
```

Your Turn! **Create your own menu files**

Create text files with menu items like Erik just did. Make sure they are *plain text* files. Try using your favorite flavors and toppings in your menus.

"Now what?" he asked his brother.

"Now let's learn how to work with files in Python. Let's create a new program for that. We'll practice a little bit, and then we'll add this code to our main program. I usually do this when I'm learning something new—I try it in a separate, simple program before adding it to the main application."

Simon continued, "Create another file in the editor and save it as files.py."

Erik had done that several times already, so it took him just a couple seconds.

"Working with files is a difficult topic, so I'll start with a diagram," Simon said.

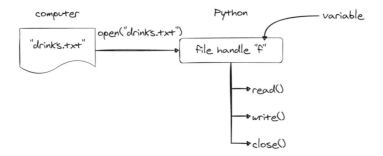

"When you work with a file in your computer, you use its name. You tell your editor program to *open* a file called `drinks.txt`. Your editor program then *reads* the file and shows you its content. Then you edit the file and save it, which means you *write* the file on the computer disk. So far, so good?" Simon asked.

"Yes," Erik said. "But disks are only used in very old computers. In my computer, it's called an SSD drive—it's not a disk anymore. My friend Alex told me."

"You're absolutely right!" Simon was glad to hear that from his brother. "Yes, it's an SSD now in most computers—it's not a disk, and it's not spinning."

"But let's get back to my files," Erik said. "I see that you wrote 'computer' and 'Python' at the top of your picture. What does that mean?"

"That means," Simon said, "that in Python, if you want to work with a file you have to create a special *object*, which is usually called a *file handle.* You use this object to read and write the file. You use a function called `open()` to create such an object. You call the `open()` function, and you pass the filename as an argument. In our case, it will be `open("drinks.txt")`. The function returns the file handle, which you put in a variable. In this case, the variable is called `f`, but you can use any name here."

"Why is it so complicated?" Erik asked. "Why can't we just use the filename?"

"Yes, it looks a bit complicated the first time. The reason for that is the filename is just a string, remember? When we want to read from the file, we want to read from *the file with that name*, not from the string. The *filename* and the file *itself* are different things. When we use the `open()` function, we create a connection between the filename and the file itself. We tell Python, 'Please find the file named `drinks.txt` inside the computer and use it *as a file*.' Don't worry too much about it right now. Sometimes the best way to understand something is to start using it."

"Okay," Erik said. He was still a bit confused about all that, but he wanted to see how he could read his menus from the text files he just created.

"Now let's write a simple Python program to work with files," Simon said. "Go to the tab in your editor where you have your `files.py` program opened. Look at my diagram: you have to call the `open()` function; pass the filename, such as `drinks.txt`; and store the result in the variable `f`. Can you write it?"

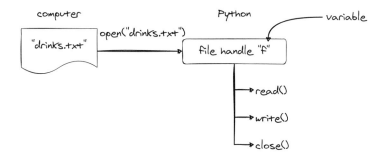

"Let me try," Erik said, and he wrote this:

```
f = open("drinks.txt")
```

"Good!" Simon said. "Now you have a file object named f, and you can read from it. To do that, you call a *method* named read(). Methods look and behave a lot like functions, but methods are applied to *objects*. We'll talk about objects later, but for now all you have to know is that to call a method of an object, you use the object's name, and then you put a dot and then the method name with parentheses, similar to calling a function, like this: f.read(). Methods also can return something, like functions, so you have to store the result somewhere. What do you think this read() method will return when you call it?"

"What's inside the file, I think," Erik answered.

"Absolutely correct!" Simon said. "Save it in a variable called drinks and then try to print it."

Erik wrote the following:

```
f = open("drinks.txt")
drinks = f.read()
print(drinks)
```

"Now run it," Simon suggested.

Erik clicked Run and got this output:

```
coffee
chocolate
decaf

>>>
```

Your Turn!   Read from a file
Write the same short program and try to read from the drinks.txt file. Make sure you can print out the whole file's content.

"It works!" He was really glad. His Python program opened a file, read it, and printed it on the page! "Now I know how to print my menus from Python. Let me write the same for the other two files."

"Right," Simon said. "But that's not exactly what we want."

"Why?" Erik couldn't understand.

"Remember, in your program, you don't just print out your menus. You also let the user choose from the menu, and then you find that item in the list, right?"

"Yes, but isn't it a list here?" Erik asked. "It looks like a list."

"It may look like a list, but it's not a list. It's a string," Simon said. "When you called the `read()` method, you copied the whole file's content into a variable called `drinks`. So this variable is just one large string. If you don't believe me, you can test it right here. See these three angle brackets in the output window? You can type any Python command here to continue working with your program—the same way we did with REPL, remember? Type `type(drinks)` here, and you'll see the type of this variable."

Erik did and saw this:

```
>>> type(drinks)
<class 'str'>
>>>
```

"You see, Python says it's a string," Simon said. "And we need a list."

"What should we do?" Erik asked.

"Luckily, Python developers knew that we might need this and created another method for the file object. It's called `readlines()`. Try changing your `read()` to `readlines()` and see what happens. Don't forget to click Stop before running your program again."

Erik changed his program to the following:

```
f = open("drinks.txt")
drinks = f.readlines()
print(drinks)
```

He clicked Stop and then Run again and got this output:

```
['coffee\n', 'chocolate\n', 'decaf\n']
>>>
```

"Try checking its type again," Simon suggested.

Erik switched to the output window and typed `type(drinks)` again:

```
>>> type(drinks)
<class 'list'>
>>>
```

> ***Your Turn!*   Check Python types**
> Repeat the checks that Erik just did. Do you see the difference between a string and a list?

"It's a list!" he said. "But what are those *slash-n* characters? I don't have them in my drinks file."

"You don't *see* them in your file, but they are there. These are *invisible* characters. When you see this *backslash-n*, it's a single character called a *newline* character. It tells the computer that it should print the next item at the beginning of the next line. Without it, all your drinks would be printed like this: `coffeechocolatedecaf`. You don't want that, right?" Simon smiled.

"Of course not!" Erik said. "But we don't need them in the list, right? I think the menu lists should look like what's in my main program, right?"

"You're absolutely right. And again, Python developers created a very useful method for that. It's called `strip()`, and it removes invisible characters from both ends of the string. We just have to apply it to every item in the list. What do you think we should use here?"

"A loop?" Erik suggested.

"Right, a loop!" Simon said. "We'll go over the list and remove those newline characters with the `strip()` method."

Simon paused for a moment, thinking. Then he continued, "There are several ways to do it. Some are shorter, but they are more difficult to understand. Let's use the one that is easier to read and follow. Actually, this is a good rule in programming: when choosing between different ways of doing something, always use the one that is easier to read and follow. If somebody is reading your code, they will thank you for that. Even yourself—if you're reading your own code three months later."

He quickly drew a diagram.

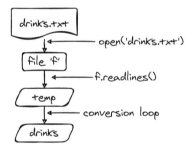

"Let's read into a temporary list from the file. Then we'll go through that temporary list, convert each item, and append it to the new list. We'll call that new list `drinks`. Then we'll repeat the same steps for flavors and toppings. We can use the same temporary variable for all of them. Let me help you," said Simon. He started typing in Erik's program. Here is what it looked like after he finished:

```
f = open("drinks.txt")
temp = f.readlines()
drinks = []
for item in temp:
```

```
    new_item = item.strip()
    drinks.append(new_item)
```

```
print(drinks)
```

He clicked Run, and they saw the result:

```
['coffee', 'chocolate', 'decaf']
>>>
```

Your Turn!   Remove the newline characters
Remove the newline characters from the menu items using the `strip()` method.

"Looks better, doesn't it?" he asked Erik. "Now go ahead and do the same thing for the other menu files."

Erik started working on his program, and when he was almost done with the `flavors.txt` file, he exclaimed, "Wait! I'm repeating myself! You told me I shouldn't repeat myself."

Simon smiled. He was happy that his little brother grasped this concept so quickly. "What should we do to *not* repeat ourselves?" he asked.

"Write a function?" Erik said.

"Yes, exactly! Look at this code: what's the same, and what's changing? What's going to be an argument, and what's this function going to return?"

Erik started thinking out loud, "I open different files, so the filename should be an argument, right?"

"Correct," Simon confirmed. "What do you want to return?"

"I think I'll return the list with menu options—after we remove those newline characters, of course. But what should I call this list?"

"You can call it anything you want because it's not *visible* from the outside. Call it `result`, for example. Then you can write `return result` at the end of the function. When you call the function, that `result` list is *assigned* to the variable in the main program, like `drinks` or `flavors`, depending on the file you're reading from. *Inside* the function, the variable will be always called `result`, but *outside* the function, in the main program, you can assign the result to any variable."

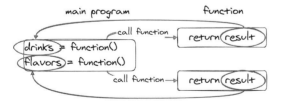

"Go ahead and write that function," Simon encouraged his brother. "Remember how to do it? Start with `def`, name the function something like `read_menu`, pass `filename` as an argument, and copy the code we just wrote."

"Okay, I'll try," Erik said. He started writing his second Python function.

Simon helped his brother a little, and here is what they wrote together:

Listing 5.4 files.py

```
def read_menu(filename):
    f = open(filename)
    temp = f.readlines()
    result = []
    for item in temp:
        new_item = item.strip()
        result.append(new_item)

    return result

drinks = read_menu("drinks.txt")
print(drinks)
flavors = read_menu("flavors.txt")
print(flavors)
toppings = read_menu("toppings.txt")
print(toppings)
```

Erik saved the file and clicked Run. Of course, he got the expected result:

```
['coffee', 'chocolate', 'decaf']
['caramel', 'vanilla', 'peppermint', 'raspberry', 'plain']
['chocolate', 'cinnamon', 'caramel']
>>>
```

> ***Your Turn!* Create a `read_menu` function**
>
> Create a `read_menu` function the same way Erik did. Make sure you don't have typos in the filenames, but what if you do? Try changing the filename and see what error Python gives you. Don't forget to fix the filename so your program works again.

"It's my second function, and it works!" he proudly said to his brother.

"Yes, you're building your own function library already—great!" Simon said. "Now let's copy your new function to the main program. Don't copy the `print()` lines—we used them just for testing. I think that file is called `menu_function.py`, right?"

"Right," Erik said. "But where should I put my function in that file? At the beginning or at the end?"

"The rule in Python is that you should define your function *before* you start using it. Because of that, functions are usually placed at the beginning of the file, before the main program. You can place it right after your first function."

"Okay," Erik said. He started working, and this is what he got:

Listing 5.5   Erik's menu with files

```
def menu(choices, title="Erik's Menu", prompt="Choose your item: "):
. . .
# this function didn't change
. . .
    return answer

def read_menu(filename):
    f = open(filename)
    temp = f.readlines()
    result = []
    for item in temp:
        new_item = item.strip()
        result.append(new_item)

    return result

drinks = read_menu("drinks.txt")
flavors = read_menu("flavors.txt")
toppings = read_menu("toppings.txt")

drink = menu(drinks)
flavor = menu(flavors, "Erik's flavors", "Choose your flavor: ")
topping = menu(toppings, "Erik's toppings", "Choose your topping: ")

print("Here is your order: ")
print("Main product: ", drink)
print("Flavor: ", flavor)
print("Topping: ", topping)
print("Thanks for your order!")
```

> ### *Your Turn!*   Copy your function to your main program
> Copy the new `read_menu()` function to your main program and try it.

He tested the program, and it worked exactly as before.

"This is good," Simon said. "Now try to add something to the toppings file. See if it changes the menu."

Erik opened the `toppings.txt` file, added 'vanilla powder' to the end of the file, and saved it. He ran the program again, and there was an additional line in the last menu: 4 `vanilla powder`.

> ### *Your Turn!*   Add another item
> Add a new item to one of the menus. Change one of the items. Don't forget to save the menu files after you change them. Check whether your program prints the updated menus.

"This is good, I like it!" Erik said. "Now anybody who can edit a text file can change the menu! Wait . . . ," he had an idea. "So I can put *anything* in these menus! Ice cream, sandwiches, or whatever! Cool, I like it! I should tell my friend Alex about it—he likes LEGO minifigures. Maybe he can use this program to exchange figures with friends!"

"Exactly right!" Simon said. "I'm glad you have so many ideas about how to use your program. This is great! I have some ideas too, but we'd better talk about them tomorrow. We also have to create the main menu tomorrow."

"What do you mean?"

"Well, currently you have to start your program every time you want to take an order. You take the order, you print it, and your program finishes. It would be better if your program could return to the initial dialogue where you ask the customer's name."

"Yes, right," Erik agreed. "It should be like a kiosk where you order something, press 'Done', and it goes to the first screen with 'Welcome to our shop'. Yes, let's do it!"

"Let's recap today's progress," Simon suggested. "What did we do today?"

"First, you said that the coffee shop manager will want to edit our menus in files. Then I wrote three files with menus for drinks, flavors, and toppings."

"Very good, what next?"

"Then I opened the files and read from them. I first read line by line, but then I had those strange 'backslash-n' characters. Then we used the `strip()` method to remove them."

"Good," Simon said. "And did you remember what I told you about objects?"

"Not really. You said that the file is an object in Python, and it's not the same as its name. And you said that functions with objects are called 'methods.'"

"Yes, that's right," Simon said. "Objects are complicated. For now we'll just use them and their methods, but we'll learn more about them later. We'll create our own objects and methods too, like we did with functions."

"Right," Erik said. "You reminded me—I wrote my second Python function, and it worked!"

"Indeed. You're becoming a serious programmer now," Simon said and smiled. "Let's take a rest for now. Tomorrow, we'll make your program even better."

New things you have learned today

- *What it means to open a file*—You have learned the difference between the file-name and the file handle inside the program.

- *What* `\n` *is and how you can remove it from strings*—You learned that the `\n` symbol means "start a new line." You don't need it in your menu items, so you used the `strip()` function to remove it.

- *What you return from a function is assigned to a variable in the main program*—You learned that the variable inside a function is not *visible* in the main program. To pass its value, you have to *return* that variable from the function and *assign* its value to another variable in the main program.

Code for this chapter

You can find the code for this chapter here: https://github.com/pavelanni/ pythonicadventure-code/tree/main/ch05.

Main menu:
Next customer!

## 6

In this chapter

- Erik creates a main menu to serve many customers
- Erik learns about Python dictionaries
- Simon explains the top-down development approach

"Yesterday, we decided that we wanted to create a main menu," Simon reminded Erik.

"Yes, you said if I wanted to use this program to serve many customers, I'd have to repeat the menus for each customer—ask their name and what they want to order."

"Exactly right!" Simon said. "And what are you going to use to do that?"

"A loop, maybe? Like we did with menus. Repeat until the customer types the right numbers or types x."

"You're absolutely right!" Simon was really glad that his brother caught on to this programming idea so quickly. "We'll ask the customer their name, like in our first program. Then we'll get their order with all the flavors and toppings."

"Yes," Erik continued, "and then we'll give them the choice to order or cancel? I saw that on some websites."

"Right. When they click Order, we save the order and print it for the barista. If they cancel, we just forget about it. In both cases, we go back to the beginning of the main menu and ask the next customer their name."

Simon took a piece of paper and started drawing. "We should first plan this algorithm visually. When we both agree how it should behave, you can start writing the code. It's always a good practice to describe a program in plain words and diagrams before you start writing any code."

"The first thing we do here is get an order," Simon said. "You see, I put it here as 'Get order'."

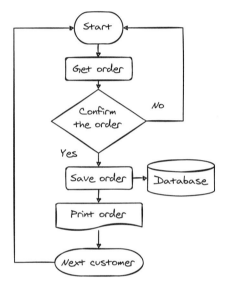

"And where are all our menus with flavors and toppings? Why didn't you put them in there?" Erik asked.

"I decided to use a block called 'Get order' that *contains* all the menus. It's common to think in big blocks first and then work on each block's details separately. This is another reason why programmers use functions. They think about the program in big blocks first and then describe each block in a separate diagram. Imagine if we included every minor detail of our program in a single diagram. It would be impossible to understand the main algorithm!"

"Let's continue," Simon said. "We get the order, and we ask the customer to confirm it. If they cancel, we return to the very first menu: 'Welcome to Erik's Coffee Shop'. But if the customer confirms the order, then we should save and print it."

"Okay, I understand that we should print it to prepare the drinks," Erik said. "But why should we save it? And what do you mean by *saving* the order?"

"First of all, it would be good at the end of the day to check how many of your friends you served in your coffee shop, don't you think?"

"But I know already," Erik said. "I prepared five drinks that day."

"But we're talking about a *real* coffee shop, don't forget. They work every day, and they serve tens and hundreds of customers. A couple of my friends worked in different coffee shops, and I can assure you, they know very well how many customers they serve each day.

"The other reason," Simon continued, "is that the coffee shop manager should know what they have in the shop and what they need to order for their inventory. Remember we talked about changing menus? Suppose they didn't order the caramel flavor in time, and they had to remove it from the menu. Why didn't they order it? Because they didn't count how many portions of caramel flavor their customers ordered. If we save all the orders and analyze them, we can order flavors and toppings before we don't have enough."

"I didn't think about that," Erik said. "Yes, it's a good idea to save the orders. But how can we do that?"

"There are several ways," Simon said. "We can use files, or we can use databases. Of course, all serious applications use databases. I think we should start with files, and then, if you're brave enough, we can use databases too."

"Yes, I want my program to be like those *serious* applications!" Erik said. "I want to try databases too!"

"Good," Simon said, "but for now let's finish with the main menu. We'll get to saving orders soon. Speaking of orders," Simon said as he took another piece of paper, "here is what's inside that 'Get order' block.

> ### *Your Turn!*   Create your own diagram
> If you decided to work on a different kind of shop, create a diagram for *your* `get_order()` function.

"We have written this function already. We just didn't call it a function. You see, we already created these dialogues to ask the customer's name, drink, flavor, and topping. There's only one thing that we haven't done yet. Do you see it?"

"Return order?" Erik asked. "We didn't do it, but I don't know what it means here."

"Here's what your order looks like, agreed?

Order:
name; Erik
drink: decaf
flavor: vanilla
topping: chocolate

"We use the function `get_order()` to collect all this information, but instead of returning four separate values for name, drink, flavor, and topping, I want to return a single *thing* that I would call an order. And that single thing contains several values that go together as a whole."

"I know, you want to use a list here!" Erik shared his insight.

"That's one of the options, but I have something better in mind. In Python, we have *dictionaries*. What is a normal dictionary?"

"It's a book with words and their meanings," Erik answered. "Or translations, if it's an English-German dictionary."

"Right!" Simon said. "You have a word, and a value that's related to the word. It could be a word and its meaning or translation, like this," and he draw a diagram.

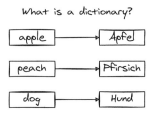

"In Python, a dictionary uses words that we call *keys* to get the *values* that are related to them. Let's look at your order. You have a key called `name`, and its value is `Erik`. You have another key called `drink`, and its value is `decaf`, and so on. The whole dictionary is called `order`, and this is what we're going to return as a result from this function.

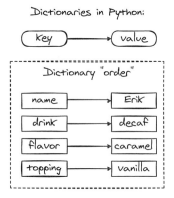

"Let's practice with REPL again," Simon suggested. "Click REPL to get to the interactive session."

Erik clicked the REPL icon and switched to the window with an interactive session. Erik's looked like this, but your version might look a little different—that's okay:

```
Jupyter QtConsole 4.7.7
Python 3.8.12 (default, Mar 12 2022, 19:58:23)
Type 'copyright', 'credits' or 'license' for more information
IPython 8.1.1 -- An enhanced Interactive Python. Type '?' for help.

In [1]:
```

"We'll start by creating an empty dictionary called `order`. To create a dictionary in Python, we use curly braces, `{}`, to make them look different from lists, which use square brackets, `[]`. Type `order = {}` and then press Enter. This will be your order."

Erik typed:

```
In [1]: order = {}

In [2]:
```

"Now we can add items to your order. Let's start with the name. Type `order['name'] = 'Erik'`. Then try to print the order with a simple `print()` function."

Erik typed:

```
In [2]: order['name'] = 'Erik'

In [3]: print(order)
 {'name': 'Erik'}

In [4]:
```

"But you said that dictionaries should use curly braces. Why do we use square brackets here?" Erik asked.

"Good question." Simon was so used to this Python feature that he couldn't find a good way to explain it right away. He started, "Well, we use curly braces to *create* a dictionary. But we use square brackets to *access* the dictionary when we want to get an item from it. In this sense, it's similar to lists—when you want to get an item from a list, you use square brackets. The difference is that with lists you use *indices* that are integer numbers. With dictionaries you use *keys* that are usually strings. If you had a normal dictionary, and you used its index—like 546—to get a word's meaning or translation, that would be inconvenient, wouldn't it? Instead, you use the word itself, like 'dog,' and finding it is fast."

"Yes, right," Erik said. "Should I add the drink, flavor, and topping now?"

"Great idea, go ahead!" Simon said.

Erik continued in his interactive session:

```
In [4]: order['drink'] = 'decaf'

In [5]: order['flavor'] = 'vanilla'

In [6]: order['topping'] = 'chocolate'

In [7]: print(order)
{'name': 'Erik', 'drink': 'decaf', 'flavor': 'vanilla',
'topping': 'chocolate'}

In [8]:
```

"Notice here," Simon said, "that your keys and values always go in pairs with a colon, :, between them."

> ### *Your Turn!*   **Learn dictionaries with REPL**
> Open REPL and work with dictionaries. You can repeat Erik's commands or create your own dictionaries. Try using different keys. Try to store a number instead of a string. Does it work?

"This is cool, I like it!" Erik said. "But can I print it in a better way, like I printed it before?"

"Of course," Simon said. "I think you should write a new function for that. But we'd better switch back to the editor."

"That will be my third function," Erik said.

"Are you still counting?" Simon smiled. "I'm sure you'll soon lose count of the functions you've written.

"Now let's start writing the main menu program in your editor," Simon continued. "We'll use a *top-down* design approach here."

"What's that?" Erik asked.

"It's like what I just showed you: first, we develop the algorithm for the whole program. We decide what the big blocks are and how we'll go from one to another. That usually includes decisions like whether you'll let users confirm or cancel the order.

"We can develop the main program and use functions like `get_order()` or `print_order()`. It doesn't matter if we don't have those functions yet. Until we write the real ones, we can write very simple functions that just print a message like 'I am a function print_order().' Some people call them *placeholders*. Then, when we see that the main menu works well and calls the right functions, we can write the real functions.

"Let me help you." Simon took the keyboard. "First, we'll create a new file and save it as `main_menu.py`. Then we'll create a new function called `main_menu()` with the `def` keyword and parentheses."

"Another function?" Erik asked.

"Yes, in programming we usually create functions for everything. The main program is usually very short, and it calls one of those functions. Then that function calls other functions, and so on. It's a good practice to write even your main menu as a function."

Simon continued, "Look at the diagram again. Do you see these arrows that go back to the 'Start'? They usually mean that in your algorithm you're going to *repeat* something. As soon as we return to the 'Start', we're going through the same algorithm again and again. And to repeat something in a program, we use . . . what?"

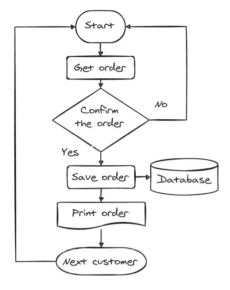

"A loop!" Erik answered.

"Exactly right!" Simon confirmed. "We used two types of loops already: a for loop and a while loop. Which one are you going to use here?"

"I think it should be a while loop," Erik said. "This main menu looks similar to what we did in the drinks menu: repeat questions and check what the user answered."

"I agree," Simon said. "Look at the code where you wrote the menu as a function. Remember, we used while True: there, and we checked what the user entered. What do you think we should check here? I'll give you a hint: on diagrams, these places where we have to make a decision are usually drawn as a diamond shape."

"I see it!" Erik said. "It's where we ask the user if they want to confirm or cancel the order."

"Okay, let's start writing it," Simon suggested.

Erik wrote:

```
def main_menu():
    while True:
```

"What's next?" he asked.

"Look at the diagram," Simon said.

"Get order?" Erik said.

"Right! And remember that the `get_order()` function will return a dictionary with the order. The dictionary will contain the customer's name, drink, flavor, and all that. We'll put that dictionary into a variable called `order` in our main menu." Simon added a line to Erik's code:

```
def main_menu():
    while True:
        order = get_order()
```

"What's next?" he asked his brother.

"Now we have to ask the customer if they confirm the order," Erik said.

"Good. But we have to show them the order before asking, I think," and Simon added a few more lines:

```
def main_menu():
    while True:
        order = get_order()
        print("Check your order:")
        print_order(order)
        confirm = input("Confirm? Press Y to confirm, N to cancel: ")
```

"Look here," Simon said to Erik, "I used the `order` variable that I received from `get_order()` as an argument for the next function, `print_order()`. This is very common in programming: we call one function to do something, it returns a result, and then we use that result as an input for another function."

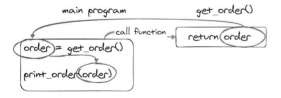

"I see," Erik said. "Like in a movie theater: the cashier prints a ticket and gives it to you. Then you take the ticket, go to the entrance, give the ticket to the attendants at the entrance, and they check it."

"Yes, good analogy, Erik! Let's continue it: we just received an answer to the question about whether the customer wants to confirm the order. Now, as you just said, we have to *check* the answer and decide what to do next. Like in a movie theater, they check if your ticket is correct and decide whether to let you in or not. Let's add these lines. Look at the diagram. If the user answers 'Yes', what should we do?"

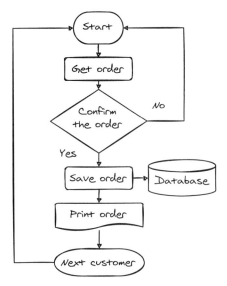

"Save and print the order," Erik answered, looking at Simon's drawing.

"Okay, and if the user wants to cancel and responds 'No'?"

"We should do nothing, just return to the beginning. But I don't know how to do it. You just have an arrow there."

"There is a simple word for this arrow in Python—continue. It means, 'Don't execute the rest of the loop, and continue the loop from the beginning.' Pretty easy, huh?" and Simon added these lines to the function:

```
def main_menu():
    while True:
        order = get_order()
        print("Check your order:")
        print_order(order)
        confirm = input("Confirm? Press Y to confirm, N to cancel: ")
        if confirm == "Y" or confirm == "y":
            save_order(order)
            print("Thanks for your order:")
            print_order(order)
        else:
            continue
```

"I see that you've added two more functions: save_order() and print_order()," Erik said. "But we haven't written them yet."

"Let's write them!" Simon exclaimed. "We'll write very simple functions for now. They will just print something like 'saving order . . . ,' so we can see that they were called. Later, we'll improve them so they do more useful things."

Simon added the functions below the `main_menu()` function:

```
def get_order():
    return {}


def print_order(order):
    print(order)
    return


def save_order(order):
    print("Saving order...")
    return
```

He explained it to Erik, "The `get_order()` function is what you have written already. We'll transfer your code here soon, but for now it does nothing. There are no menus and no dialogue, but it has to return the order. Remember, the order will be a dictionary with keys like 'name' and 'drink', but for now the function just returns an empty dictionary, which is a pair of curly braces. So far, so good?"

"Yes," Erik answered. "So you mean we'll copy my previous functions from that previous file into this one, right?"

"Right," Simon said. "Sometimes when a program becomes larger, it's a good idea to group functions in separate files. But in our case, it's easier to keep everything in one file.

"The `print_order()` function," Simon continued, "just prints the order that it gets from the argument. In this case, we'll use the standard Python `print()` function, but we'll make it prettier later. You've done that already, remember?"

"Sure!" Erik said. "I think we can make it look like a real coffee shop receipt."

"Good idea," Simon said. "The `save_order()` function does nothing except print 'Saving order . . .'. That's okay for now—we'll write it later.

"Now we're ready to call the `main_menu()` function and test our algorithm. Go ahead and add the call for `main_menu()` at the end and run it. Your main program will consist of only this function call."

Erik added the function call, so the whole program now looked like this:

Listing 6.1   A main menu with simple functions

```
def main_menu():
    while True:
        order = get_order()
        print("Check your order:")
        print_order(order)
        confirm = input("Confirm? Press Y to confirm, N to cancel: ")
```

```
        if confirm == "Y" or confirm == "y":
            save_order(order)
            print("Thanks for your order:")
            print_order(order)
        else:
            continue


def get_order():
    return {}


def print_order(order):
    print(order)
    return


def save_order(order):
    print("Saving order...")
    return

main_menu()
```

Your Turn!   **Create a main menu**
Write a main menu function similar to the one Erik just created. Feel free to change the dialogue messages.

He clicked Run and saw this output:

```
Check your order:
{}
Confirm? Press Y to confirm, N to cancel:
```

He typed y and got this:

```
Saving order...
Thanks for your order:
{}
Check your order:
{}
Confirm? Press Y to confirm, N to cancel: y
```

"Why does it give me the 'Check your order' again?" Erik asked.

"Because it's a loop!" Simon said. "After you answered y to the confirmation question, it returns to the beginning of the loop. And because we haven't added your menu dialogue yet, it prints an empty order. Everything works as expected. Now try answering n to the question."

Erik typed `n` and got this output:

```
Confirm? Press Y to confirm, N to cancel: n
 Check your order:
{}
Confirm? Press Y to confirm, N to cancel:
```

"Do you see the difference?" Simon asked.

"I see that it didn't print 'Saving order . . .' this time. That means it followed the short arrow on the right side of your diagram."

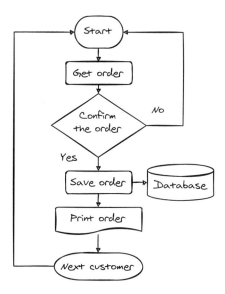

"Excellent!" Simon was glad to see that Erik really understood his algorithm diagram.

"I think we made good progress today—our main menu is working. Tomorrow we'll write the actual functions that will do what we want. For now, let's wrap up and review what you learned today."

"We used the `while` loop again!" Erik said.

"Right! And you used what you've learned while working on menus," Simon confirmed.

"Also, we learned about dictionaries. They are like normal dictionaries, but you can store anything there, not just word descriptions."

"Yes, exactly! In our simple `order` dictionary, we keep names, drinks, and flavors. But in a more complex dictionary, you can keep numbers—prices, for example—and even lists and other dictionaries. Dictionaries are really useful in Python, and you'll use them all the time."

"Also, I liked how you created simple functions just to test the main menu," Erik said. "You said it's called 'top-down,' right?"

"Exactly," Simon said. "There is also a 'bottom-up' approach, as you could guess. In that case, people create functions first, test them properly, and then combine them into a large program. In some sense, we used this approach too, when you created and tested your first `menu()` function. Now we're going to use your function in our large program.

"Time to take a rest now," Simon continued. "Tomorrow, we'll work on the functions we put in our main menu."

New things you have learned today

- *Top-down approach*—First you develop the "big picture" of your application and use simple functions that just print something instead of doing real work. When the main algorithm works properly, you develop the actual functions.
- *Dictionary*—In Python, dictionaries can store pairs of keys and values. You can assign values to keys, and you can quickly find them with their keys.
- *Flowchart diagram symbols*—Programmers usually use diagrams to discuss their algorithms before they start writing code. Usually, a rectangle means some process, and a diamond shape means a decision point with a Yes/No question. There are also symbols for input, using documents, using databases, and others. We'll introduce them later.

Code for this chapter

You can find the code for this chapter here: https://github.com/pavelanni/pythonicadventure-code/tree/main/ch06.

Creating functions:
Get the order and print it

7

In this chapter

- Erik creates the actual functions to get and print orders
- Erik uses a dictionary to store and print a customer's order
- Erik's program now works as planned!
- Erik and Simon plan to write a function to save orders

"Yesterday, we created the main menu, right?" Simon began his conversation with Erik. "We even tested the main menu's functionality."

"Yes, but it didn't do anything useful," Erik said.

"Right!" Simon said. "Remember, we talked about the 'top-down' approach? We created empty functions just to test the main menu. Now it's time to make them do something real. Open your Python file where we created menus from files. It's called `menu_files.py`."

Erik opened that file, and now he had two tabs in his editor: one with the `main_menu.py` file and another with the `menu_files.py` file.

"Switch to the `main_menu.py` file, and let's look at which functions we have to write there," Simon said. "There are three functions: `get_order()`, `print_order()`, and `save_order()`. Let's begin with `get_order()`. Where is our diagram?"

"Let's start with `get_name`. What do we do here?" Simon asked.

"We just ask 'What's your name?'," Erik answered.

"Right, and then?"

"And then we save it in a variable, like `name`."

"Almost right," Simon said. "Remember, we decided that `order` will be a dictionary. And we'll save *everything* related to that order in this dictionary. For example, to save the customer's name, instead of `name = 'Erik'`, we should write `order['name'] = 'Erik'`. Only, instead of 'Erik', we'll use the `input()` function, like you did in your first program."

"Let me try," Erik said. He wrote this function:

```
def get_order():
    order['name'] = input("What's your name: ")
    return {}
```

"Now try it," Simon said.

Erik clicked Run. The program asked his name, and he entered 'Erik'. But then he got several lines of error messages:

```
What's your name: Erik
 Traceback (most recent call last):
  File "/home/erik/mu_code/main_menu.py", line 41, in <module>
    main_menu()
  File "/home/erik/mu_code/main_menu.py", line 3, in main_menu
    order = get_order()
  File "/home/erik/mu_code/main_menu.py", line 27, in get_order
```

```
    order['name'] = input("What's your name: ")
NameError: name 'order' is not defined
>>>
```

"What's that?" he asked Simon.

"Look, Python tells you where your problem is occurring. Read the last line."

"Name 'order' is not defined," Erik read.

"It's very simple," Simon explained. "You tried to put something in the dictionary, but you haven't created it yet. That's easy to fix. Let's create an empty dictionary. Remember, we use curly braces for that. Just write `order = {}` before the line with `input()`."

Erik changed his function to this:

```
def get_order():
    order = {}
    order['name'] = input("What's your name: ")
    return {}
```

He ran it again, and this time it didn't give him any errors:

```
What's your name: Erik
 Check your order:
{}
Confirm? Press Y to confirm, N to cancel: y
 Saving order...
Thanks for your order:
{}
What's your name:
```

"It's better now," he said.

"Yes, better, but look: it still prints an empty order. You created an order and even entered your name, but your function returns an empty dictionary. See this line: `return {}`?"

"But that's how *you* wrote it!" Erik was sure this wasn't his fault.

"Yes, I wrote it that way to test the main menu function. But now we have to return the actual `order` dictionary. Change it to `return order`, and let's see if it prints your name."

Erik changed the function:

```
def get_order():
    order = {}
    order['name'] = input("What's your name: ")
    return order
```

And he ran it again. This time it printed his name:

```
What's your name: Erik
 Check your order:
{'name': 'Erik'}
Confirm? Press Y to confirm, N to cancel:
```

"Yes, it prints my name now!"

"Congratulations!" Simon said. "Now you know how to work with dictionaries."

Your Turn! **Create a `get_order()` function**

Start writing your own `get_order()` function in the `main_menu.py` file. Add the first input to get the customer's name. Test it by running the main menu program.

What are your choices?

"Let's move on," Simon continued. "We have to add your `menu()` function now to list drinks and flavors. But we also need the `read_menu()` function to read your menus from files. Copy both `menu()` and `read_menu()` from the `menu_files.py` file and paste them here in `main_menu.py`. Paste them right before the `def get_order():` line."

"What if I paste them after that line?" Erik wanted to know why his older brother gave him such strict orders.

"Then it won't work." Simon gave him a simple answer and smiled. "Okay, if you *really* want to know, we are going to use these two functions in the `get_order()` function. First, we have to read the menu contents from the files: your drinks, flavors, and toppings. Then we call the `menu()` function three times to get the customer choices. And before we can use these functions, we should *define* them.

"In other words, we should tell Python that these functions exist and what they do. That's why they need to be pasted before the `def get_order():` line. By the way, this is why we use the word `def` to start a function—we *define* it."

"Okay," Erik said. He started copying the functions. In a couple of moments his `main_menu.py` file looked like this:

Listing 7.1 The main menu is ready

```python
def main_menu():
    while True:
        order = get_order()
        print("Check your order:")
        print_order(order)
        confirm = input("Confirm? Press Y to confirm, N to cancel: ")
        if confirm == "Y" or confirm == "y":
            save_order(order)
            print("Thanks for your order:")
            print_order(order)
        else:
            continue

def menu(choices, title="Erik's Menu", prompt="Choose your item: "):
    print(title)
    print(len(title) * "-")
    i = 1
    for c in choices:
```

```
            print(i, c)
            i = i + 1
        while True:
            choice = input(prompt)
            allowed_answers = []
            for a in range(1, len(choices) + 1):
                allowed_answers.append(str(a))

            allowed_answers.append("X")
            allowed_answers.append("x")

            if choice in allowed_answers:
                if choice == "X" or choice == "x":
                    answer = ""
                    break
                else:
                    answer = choices[int(choice) - 1]
                    break
            else:
                print("Enter number from 1 to ", len(choices))
                answer = ""
        return answer

def read_menu(filename):
    f = open(filename)
    temp = f.readlines()
    result = []
    for item in temp:
        new_item = item.strip()
        result.append(new_item)
    return result
# . . .
#  No changes in get_order() and save_order() functions
# . . .
main_menu()
```

"Correct!" Simon said. "Now you know the rule: define something before using it. You already saw the errors you got when you didn't define the order dictionary.

"Now we are ready to use these functions in get_order()," he continued. "Look at your menu_files.py program. What did we do first?"

"We read the menus from files," Erik answered.

"Good. Let's do that here, but inside the function."

Erik added three lines to the get_order() function:

```
def get_order():
    order = {}
    order["name"] = input("What's your name: ")
    drinks = read_menu("drinks.txt")
    flavors = read_menu("flavors.txt")
    toppings = read_menu("toppings.txt")
    return order
```

He had to add four spaces before each line so they were all indented at the same level.

"And now the same with three `menu()` functions?" he asked Simon.

"Sure, go ahead!"

Erik changed his function to this:

```
def get_order():
    order = {}
    order["name"] = input("What's your name: ")
    drinks = read_menu("drinks.txt")
    flavors = read_menu("flavors.txt")
    toppings = read_menu("toppings.txt")
    drink = menu(drinks, "Erik's drinks", "Choose your drink: ")
    flavor = menu(flavors, "Erik's flavors", "Choose your flavor: ")
    topping = menu(toppings, "Erik's toppings", "Choose your topping: ")
    return order
```

He was proud of his work and looked at Simon.

"Almost right," Simon said. "You copied it right, but you need to change the code a bit to store the answers in the `order` dictionary. It should be an easy change—you know how to do it."

"Ah, I see," Erik said. He changed the function. Now it looked like this:

Listing 7.2 main_menu.py

```
def get_order():
    order = {}
    order["name"] = input("What's your name: ")
    drinks = read_menu("drinks.txt")
    flavors = read_menu("flavors.txt")
    toppings = read_menu("toppings.txt")
    order["drink"] = menu(drinks, "Erik's drinks",
                          "Choose your drink: ")
    order["flavor"] = menu(flavors, "Erik's flavors",
                           "Choose your flavor: ")
    order["topping"] = menu(toppings, "Erik's toppings",
                            "Choose your topping: ")
    return order
```

Simon encouraged him, "Go ahead, run it!"

Erik ran the program.

```
What's your name: Erik
 Erik's drinks
 -------------
1 coffee
2 chocolate
3 decaf
Choose your drink: 1
 Erik's flavors
 -------------
1 caramel
```

```
2 vanilla
3 peppermint
4 raspberry
5 plain
Choose your flavor: 2
 Erik's toppings
 --------------
1 chocolate
2 cinnamon
3 caramel
4 vanilla powder
Choose your topping: 3
 Check your order:
{'name': 'Erik', 'drink': 'coffee', 'flavor': 'vanilla',
'topping': 'caramel'}
Confirm? Press Y to confirm, N to cancel: y
 Saving order...
Thanks for your order:
{'name': 'Erik', 'drink': 'coffee', 'flavor': 'vanilla',
'topping': 'caramel'}
What's your name:
```

"Wow!" He was really happy. "I wrote a program of more than 70 lines, and it works!"

"Yes, you did—it really works," Simon confirmed and smiled.

> **Your Turn!   Add menu choices to your program**
>
> Add the menu() and read_menu() functions like in the preceding program to your main_menu.py file. Test the program by running it and entering your choices. Try entering wrong choices, and make sure the menu() function doesn't allow you to do it.

Print it!

"But something is still missing. The order doesn't look very professional. It doesn't look like a real coffee shop," Simon continued.

"I see. We should change the print_order() function, right?" Erik suggested.

"Yes, right. Go to the print_order() function in your main_menu.py file."

Erik's print_order() function looked like this:

```
def print_order(order):
    print(order)
    return
```

"Here we use the default printing function provided by Python," Simon continued. "Python *can* print your dictionary, but it's not pretty. It's okay for debugging, but for real orders and receipts, we have to make it more beautiful. You have done that already, right?"

"You mean, when I printed lines of dashes? Yes, it was prettier than this."

"Let's do something similar to what you did at the end of the `menu_files.py` file. You can copy those lines, starting with `print`, from there. Just remember to keep the right indentation, and make sure you use the dictionary and not simple variables. And don't forget that we now have the customer's name. I think you should use it in your function. Ready?"

"Yes," Erik answered. He started working on the function. He ended up with this:

```
def print_order(order):
    print("Here is your order, ", order["name"])
    print("Main product: ", order["drink"])
    print("Flavor: ", order["flavor"])
    print("Topping: ", order["topping"])
    print("Thanks for your order!")
    return
```

> ***Your Turn!***   **Add a `print_order()` function**
>
> Add a `print_order()` function to the `main_menu.py` file. Feel free to use decorations like dashes (-), underscores (_), or equal signs (=) to make your printed order look like the ones you've seen somewhere else. Try to find receipts from restaurants, coffee shops, or ice cream shops, and see if you can make yours look similar.

He ran the program again and got much prettier output:

```
Here is your order,  Erik
Main product:  coffee
Flavor:  vanilla
Topping:  caramel
Thanks for your order!
Confirm? Press Y to confirm, N to cancel:
```

"Yes, this is much better!" Simon said. "You can add decorations like dashes and vertical lines—it's up to you. But you did a great job as a programmer. You wrote several very useful functions, you organized them properly, and you tested them. Good job, Erik. I'm really proud of you!"

"Also, we learned about dictionaries, and I used them." Erik sensed that it was wrap-up time, and he should mention everything he learned and used that day.

"Yes, right," Simon confirmed. "Dictionaries are very important in Python. We use them all the time in our programs. Later, you'll learn more about them."

"You said we should also save our orders somehow. Will we do it tomorrow?" Erik asked.

"Yes, sure," Simon said. "Do you know about JSON?" he asked.

"Jason? Yes, we are in math class together. What about him?"

"No, not that Jason," Simon laughed. "JSON is a file format that we can use to save your coffee shop orders. We'll talk about it tomorrow, okay?"

"Okay," Erik said. And off he went.

New things you have learned today

- *Variable and function definitions*—In Python, we have to *define* variables and functions before we can use them. For variables, this is as simple as assigning an empty value to the variable. For a dictionary, it's `order = {}`, and for a string, it's `name = ""`. Functions should be defined using the `def` keyword.

Code for this chapter

You can find the code for this chapter here: https://github.com/pavelanni/pythonicadventure-code/tree/main/ch07.

Working with JSON: Save the order

"You said something about Jason, yesterday," Erik asked Simon. "But you said it's another Jason, not the one from my math class."

"Yes, that's another Jason," Simon smiled. "It's JSON, J–S–O–N, the file format we use to store data."

"Like the files we used to store menus?"

"Yes, similar," Simon answered. "But this format is very good for storing *structured* data."

"What's that?" Erik asked.

"Sometimes you want to store just a piece of text or an image. They usually don't have any fixed structure. Text is just text. And an image can be large or small, it can

be black and white or color, but it doesn't have any structure—it's just a bunch of pixels. This is what we call *unstructured* data.

"But in your case, each order has a *structure*. Each order has the customer's name
and all the components of the drink you're going to prepare—no more, no less. It
always has the main drink, the flavor, and the topping. Because of the menu you
wrote, the customer should answer all these questions before you can print or save the
order. Also, the customer can't *add* anything to the order."

"Like another topping?" Erik asked.

"Yes," Simon said. "You order is an example of *structured* data."

Erik didn't think that he had created something with such a serious name.

"Your order is stored in a dictionary," Simon continued, "and you know for sure
that for each order there are dictionary *keys* (Remember what those are?) called `name`,
`drink`, `flavor`, and `topping`." Simon pulled out one of his diagrams.

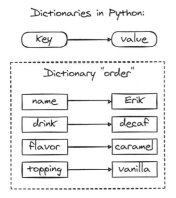

"The JSON format is created to store this kind of structured data. Let's practice with it
a little. Like before, we'll create a simple program first and try some simple operations. Then we'll take what we've learned in this simple program and use it to make
our main program save orders in a file. That's a lot for one day, so maybe we'll do
some of it tomorrow."

Simon continued, "Now open your editor and create a new file. Save it with the
name `dict_json.py`, for example."

Erik opened his editor window and clicked New. He then clicked Save, entered
`dict_json.py`, and clicked Save again. He was already familiar with the procedure.

"Now," Simon said, "create an example order."

"What is an example order?"

"Your order is a dictionary, right?" Simon started to explain. "In your main program, you created an empty dictionary and then started to fill it with the values you
were getting from the customer. Here, we want to skip that step and imagine that our
`order` dictionary is already filled with the customer's choices. Let me start it for you,"
Simon said. He typed in Erik's editor:

```
order = {
    "name": "Erik",
```

"You can continue," he said. "Don't forget to close the curly braces."

Erik finished the `order` dictionary and closed the curly braces. Now it looked like this:

```
order = {
    "name": "Erik",
    "drink": "coffee",
    "flavor": "caramel",
    "topping": "chocolate"
    }
```

"I noticed that you indented the lines in this dictionary," he said to his brother. "Is that a rule for dictionaries in Python?"

"No," Simon answered. "In this case, I did it just to make it look better. And to make it more *readable*. I could put all the items together in one line, or start from the beginning of the line, but I think it looks better this way.

"Now," he continued, "we have a dictionary. And we want to save it in a file. I guess I should remind you about file operations with dictionaries."

"Yes," Erik said. "It was *so* long ago. I don't remember much."

"Sure," Simon said. "Also, you'll learn a couple of new things about files. First, we have to *open* a file. To open a file, we need to call a function named `open()`—of course—and pass the filename as an argument. You know everything about functions and their arguments, right?

"The `open()` function returns a file *handle*. It's a special object that our program can use to work with that file."

Simon wrote one more line below the dictionary that Erik had created:

```
order = {
    "name": "Erik",
    "drink": "coffee",
    "flavor": "caramel",
    "topping": "chocolate"
    }

f = open("orders.json", "w")
```

"Here is the first new thing. See this `w` in the last line? It means that we're going to write into the file."

"But when we opened the menu files, we didn't use any letters," Erik remembered.

"You're right!" Simon said. "We didn't use any letters—they are called *modes*, by the way—because when we don't use any letters, Python opens files for reading. This time, we want to write to this file, so we need to tell Python about it."

"And I see that you named the file 'orders.json'. Is it because you want to use that JSON format you were talking about?"

"Yes, exactly," Simon answered. "It's not mandatory, but it's a convention to add the `.json` extension to JSON files. Another difference with 'write' mode is that Python will create a file with this name if it doesn't already exist."

"What next?" Erik asked. "How do we write to this JSON file? Last time we used 'methods'—is that what they're called?"

"Yes, you remembered correctly," Simon said. "But this time we'll do it differently. This is all because we're going to write structured data, not just plain text. We're going to use a Python *module* called `json`."

"What's a module?" Erik asked immediately.

"I'll explain it right now," Simon said. He smiled. "Remember, you wrote several Python functions recently. For example, the one that reads menu items from a file and returns a list. Imagine one of your friends wanted to write their own program for a coffee shop or something similar."

"Yes," Erik said. "I spoke with Emily recently, and she said she wanted to create a program for an ice cream shop."

"Great!" Simon said. "You may want to help her and share the functions that you wrote. It will save her some time, so her program will be ready earlier. It's very common among programmers to share their work to help each other. In Python, you can group functions that you want to share in a file and give it to Emily. She can copy that file to her computer and then *import* it into her program. After she has imported it, she can use your functions in her application. Your file with functions is called a *module.*"

"What if I don't want to share my functions?" Erik asked. "I spent several days writing them!"

"Yes, you did," Simon said. "And you did a great job. But remember, a lot of people spent many days writing other functions in Python, and even Python itself. They shared their work with other programmers, so you can use Python and other functions completely free. That way, we help each other to work on our projects. It would be much slower if you and I had to write everything ourselves from scratch. That's why people use someone else's code and share their code with others. It's usually called the *open source community.*"

"Back to JSON," Simon continued. "We're going to use the module called `json`, written by other people. That module can read Python dictionaries and convert them to JSON files. Go to the beginning of your file and add a line: `import json`. It should be the very first line of the file."

Erik did. Here is his updated file:

```
import json

order = {
    "name": "Erik",
    "drink": "coffee",
    "flavor": "caramel",
    "topping": "chocolate"
    }

f = open("orders.json", "w")
```

"Now we have to convert your example order to JSON and write it to the file we just opened," Simon said. "In the json module, this function is called dump. We'll call it in your program, but we have to tell Python that it should look for this function in the json module, so we call it like this: json.dump(). You just have to pass two arguments: the dictionary and the file object. Add this function to the end of the file. Your dictionary is order, your file object is f."

Erik added this line to the end of the program:

```
json.dump(order, f)
```

Simon continued, "There is another thing that we didn't do with files before. We should *close* the file. This is important, so let's look at another diagram.

"Here are three main components of a computer: the processor, the memory, and the drive. Your Python program is running on the processor. Your file is stored on the drive in a filesystem. A filesystem is what you see in Finder on a Mac. In Explorer on Windows, it's folders and files. When you want to work with a file in Python, you *open* it, like you already did. That creates a file object in your program. When you write to the file, you write to the computer memory. Then, when you want your file to be *really* written to the filesystem on the drive, you *close* it."

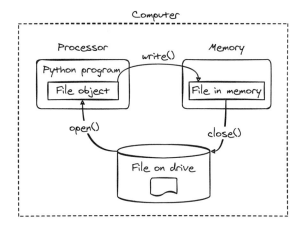

"This is so complicated!" Erik was confused. "Why don't we write straight to the drive?"

"Computers *are* complicated, you're right!" Simon agreed. "The reason is that computer engineers try to make computers work faster. Writing to a drive is slow—much slower than writing to memory. Imagine you're writing your program in a text editor. If it saved every letter you typed immediately to the drive, it would be *very* slow. You don't like working with slow computers, do you?"

"I hate slow computers!" Erik answered.

"To make computers work faster," Simon continued, "engineers decided to store data in memory and to save it to the drive only when necessary. There are a lot of tricks they use to make computers run faster, and, of course, I don't know all of them. Maybe I'll learn more about them in college.

"Let's get back to our program and close the file. Remember, file objects use methods. In this case, we call `f.close()`. That will make sure our order is written to the file. Add it after the last line in your program."

That was easy after such a long explanation. Erik added it quickly and got this:

```
import json

order = {
    "name": "Erik",
    "drink": "coffee",
    "flavor": "caramel",
    "topping": "chocolate"
    }

f = open("orders.json", "w")
json.dump(order, f)
f.close()
```

"Now run it," Simon said.

Erik clicked Run and saw the familiar >>> at the bottom of the window. "Now what?" he asked Simon.

"Nothing happened?" Simon smiled. He felt Erik's confusion. "That's because you didn't tell Python to print anything. But still, something happened behind the scenes. Python opened a file called `orders.json`, wrote your order into it, and closed it. Now we have to open it to check if it wrote it right. Use a plain text editor to open the file. You're on a Mac, so it will be TextEdit from your Applications folder. On Windows it's Notepad, and on Linux it's gedit or Kate. Start the editor and open the file. It's in your home folder, under `mu_code`, and it's called `orders.json`."

Erik started TextEdit, found the file, and opened it. Indeed, he saw his order.

```
● ● ●                          orders.json
{"name": "Erik", "drink": "coffee", "flavor": "caramel", "topping": "chocolate"}
```

> **Your Turn!   Save your example order in a JSON file**
> Write the program Erik just wrote. Try creating a slightly different example order. Run the program and check the resulting JSON file with a text editor. Try creating a different order and run the program again. Did your JSON file change? (You may have to reload the file in your text editor.)

"You see?" Simon asked. "It's your example order stored in a file. Let me add something, and you'll see why JSON files are ideal for storing Python dictionaries."

Simon took the keyboard and changed the `json.dump()` call to this:

```
json.dump(order, f, indent=4)
```

He ran the program again and re-opened the `orders.json` file. It looked familiar to Erik.

```
●  ●  ●                                    orders.json
{
    "name": "Erik",
    "drink": "coffee",
    "flavor": "caramel",
    "topping": "chocolate"
}
```

> ### *Your Turn!*   **Make it beautiful**
> Add the `indent=4` argument to your previous program, run the program again, and check if your JSON file has changed.

"It looks exactly like my dictionary!" Erik exclaimed.

"I told you," Simon said. "We'll be using JSON to store your orders. I said 'orders,' which means now we have to learn how to keep several orders and store them in a file. We know already how Python stores several items in order—you used that for your menus."

"A list!" Erik said.

"Correct! A list in Python can contain different things: strings, numbers, even dictionaries. In this case, we'll have a list of dictionaries. Each dictionary will contain an order, and we'll add them one by one to the list—a new customer, a new order, a new dictionary. I'll draw a diagram.

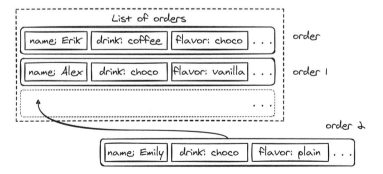

"Let's create a list of orders," Simon continued. "Copy the existing order in the code and call it `order1`, for example.

"Then change the order's content: the name, the drink, and the other choices."

Erik worked on his code for a while and created this additional order, just below the first one:

```
order1 = {
    "name": "Alex",
    "drink": "choco",
    "flavor": "vanilla",
    "topping": "caramel"
}
```

"Good," Simon said. "Now create an empty list called `orders`. Note that it's plural—`orders`. This is very similar to creating an empty dictionary—you have done that already—just instead of curly braces, use square brackets."

Erik added the following line below the second order:

```
orders = []
```

"Now we'll add both orders to the list," Simon said. "Believe it or not, the `orders` list that you just created is also an object. In Python, everything is an object, and each object has methods that you can use. You just have to know what methods exist for each object. For example, for all lists, there is a method called `append()`. It adds the element you pass as an argument to the end of the list.

"Look, I'll use it to add `order` and `order1` to the list `orders`." Simon added these two lines below the line where the `orders` list was created:

```
orders.append(order)
orders.append(order1)
```

"But how do you know that you should use `append()` here?" Erik asked.

"I read it in the Python documentation when I learned Python," Simon answered with a smile. "You can use Google to search for 'Python list methods,' and you'll find everything you need to know.

"Now we can try to save this list as JSON," Simon continued. "The only thing we need to change is *what* we want to 'dump' into the file. We used `order` as an argument for the `dump()` function to write one order. Now let's replace it with `orders` (plural!) and see what changes."

Erik changed the line with `json.dump()` to this:

```
json.dump(orders, f, indent=4)
```

He ran the program and opened the `orders.json` file again.

```
● ◉ ●                                  🗋 orders.json
|[
    {
        "name": "Erik",
        "drink": "coffee",
        "flavor": "caramel",
        "topping": "chocolate"
    },
    {
        "name": "Alex",
        "drink": "chocolate",
        "flavor": "vanilla",
        "topping": "caramel"
    }
]
```

> ### Your Turn! Save a list
> Add another example order and call it `order2`. Create a list of orders, and save the list in the same JSON file. Check the result with a text editor. Add as many more orders as you can think of and write them out to the file. Is there any limit to how many orders you can save?

"So, what do you say?" Simon asked. "Does it look like your orders?"

"Yes, it's exactly like Python!" Erik said. "But why did we write my orders in a separate file? If it looks like Python, why don't we write my orders into our Python program?"

"Great question!" Simon was really glad that Erik wanted to understand things. "First of all, we always want to separate programs from data. Remember, when you run your Word application, you don't write your documents into the Word program. You save them in separate files. That's exactly what we're doing here. Your program could save orders in different files, for example, for different days. All you'd have to do is change the name of the output file, such as `orders.Monday.json`, `orders.Tuesday.json`, and so on.

"The second reason," Simon continued, "is that this format is called JSON for a reason. It stands for JavaScript Object Notation. It was invented by people who used the JavaScript programming language, and then other languages started using it. So you can use Python to write your orders in a JSON file, and then some of your friends could create another program in JavaScript that would read from that file and print your orders on a web page, for example."

"Yes, I heard some people in my class say they know JavaScript," Erik said.

"Good! You may want to create a programming team and work on applications together," Simon said.

"But let's continue with our program. Now we'll read the orders from the JSON file and save them into a new list. Let's call it `saved_orders`."

"Why are we reading it if we just wrote it to the file?" Erik was confused.

"Maybe I didn't explain it properly," Simon answered. "In this program, we're practicing some operations with JSON files, so we know them well and can use them in our main program. Programmers do this often: they create simple programs to test concepts and ideas. Let me show you my plan for our main program, so you better understand where we're going."

Simon took another piece of paper and started drawing.

"First, we check if the file called `orders.json` exists. If it exists, we open it and read our previous orders from it."

"Why do we need our previous orders? We have prepared them already," Erik asked.

"Yes, but remember, we may want to count how many customers we served today, yesterday, or last month. Or count how many portions of caramel we have used and decide if it's time to buy more. You need all the orders if you want to manage your coffee shop business seriously. That's why all businesses keep these records for a long time."

"What if we don't have this file?" Erik asked.

"That means we have just opened our business and started working," Simon said. "In this case, we'll create an empty list and start getting orders. The file will be created automatically when we open it for writing.

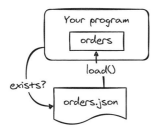

"Look at this diagram: here, we have our `orders` list either filled with our previous days' orders, or the list is empty. As we start getting orders we save them to this list. After we're done for the day, we close the file, and that saves all our orders on the drive. The next day, we open the file again and continue taking orders. All the new orders will be added to the previous day's orders."

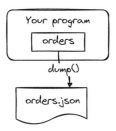

Your Turn!   Draw your own diagrams
Try to draw diagrams for your program without looking in the book. Drawing diagrams will help you understand how programs work.

"Is this how real coffee shops work? Like *Starbucks*?" Erik asked.

"Yes, pretty much," Simon said. "Of course, they use a database for reliability and security. Their order records are also more complex than ours. But the whole process is very similar.

"Now that you know the grand plan, let's continue with our simple program and read from the file. We'll read the previous orders into a new list called `saved_orders`, and then we'll print it to see if we read it correctly. To do that, there is a function called `load()` in the `json` module. It works the same way as `dump()`: first, we open a file, but this time for reading, not writing. Then we call `json.load()` and pass the file object as an argument. The function *returns* the object it read from the file, and we assign that object to a variable. In our case, it will be a list of orders, which are dictionaries, as you'll remember.

"Sound complicated? Let me help you. It's much shorter in Python." Simon started adding lines to Erik's code. Here is what he added at the end of the program:

```
f = open("orders.json", "r")
saved_orders = json.load(f)
print(saved_orders)
```

He clicked Run, and Erik saw the output.

```
Running: dict_json.py
[{'name': 'Erik', 'drink': 'coffee', 'flavor': 'caramel', 'topping': 'chocolate'}, {'name': 'Alex', 'drink':
'chocolate', 'flavor': 'vanilla', 'topping': 'caramel'}]
>>>
```

> ### *Your Turn!*   Read from the JSON file
> Add the preceding lines to your program and try to read from the JSON file you created. Do you get the same orders as in your example orders?

"You learned a lot today," Simon said. "Let's take a break until tomorrow. Then we'll add these functions to our main program, and it'll become a real Coffee Shop application. Can you quickly recap what we did today?"

"We created a JSON file from my Python dictionary, and it looked very much like Python. Then you explained all about files, memory, and drives. We also created a list of dictionaries and saved it in the file too."

"And we learned about Python modules and how to import them," Simon added. "So far, so good," he said. "Let's continue tomorrow. We're very close to finishing the first version of your application."

New things you have learned today

- *JSON (JavaScript Object Notation)*—A format that is used to store structured data and that can be used to exchange information between programs.
- *Python modules*—Groups of Python functions that can be used by other programmers. Usually, they are grouped in files. You have to `import` modules before using them.
- *Lists of dictionaries*—Lists can contain different types: strings, numbers, dictionaries, and even other lists.
- *File operations*—You can open files for reading and writing. You can write data to files, but it's written in the computer's memory. You should close the files to save the data onto the computer's drive.
- *Open source community*—People who share programs they write and help each other write better code.

Code for this chapter

You can find the code for this chapter here: https://github.com/pavelanni/pythonicadventure-code/tree/main/ch08.

Complete the menu: A real program

In this chapter

- Erik and Simon create load and save functions in the main program
- Simon adds exit functions to the main menu and `get_order()` function
- Simon explains why he thinks Erik just created a real program
- The brothers discuss future plans

"Now let's get real," Simon said. "Yesterday, we played with sample orders and simple programs. Today, it's time to use what you learned in your real program."

"Yes, let's do it!" Erik said.

"Open your `main_menu.py` file, where you wrote the main menu. We should add a couple of functions there to work with the JSON file. Let's recall what we have to do first." Simon pulled out his diagram from yesterday.

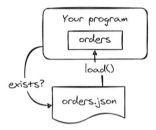

"We have to write a function that will load the list of orders from a JSON file. But first, it has to check if the file exists. If the file doesn't exist, we'll create an empty list and return it from this function. If the file exists, we'll read from it, convert the JSON file to a Python list, and return that list.

"Let me help you." Simon felt that it might be a bit confusing for Erik. "Usually, in functions that work with files, we pass the filename as an argument." Simon started the function at the bottom of the file, right before the last line with `main_menu()`:

```
def load_orders(filename):
```

"Now we have to check if the file exists. There is a special function for that, and we can find it in the `os` module."

"What is 'os'?" Erik asked.

"OS stands for 'operating system.' The operating system in the computer manages all the files and programs. It works with your screen, your keyboard, your speakers, and your video camera. On a typical computer, the OS can be Windows, macOS, or Linux.

"We're going to ask the operating system if a file with such a name exists on this computer." Simon added a line:

```
def load_orders(filename):
    if os.path.exists(filename):
```

"Look, we used the `os` module here. That means we have to import it the same way you imported the `json` module in your sample program yesterday. In this program, we haven't imported the `json` or `os` modules yet, so let's import them both."

Simon moved the cursor to the very beginning of the file and added two lines:

```
import os
import json
```

He returned the cursor to the `load_orders()` function at the end of the file and continued his explanation. "If the file exists, we open it for reading. Then we use the `json.load()` function to read from the file to the list `orders` and return the list." He added three lines to the function:

```
def load_orders(filename):
    if os.path.exists(filename):
        f = open(filename, "r")
        orders = json.load(f)
        return orders
```

"If it doesn't exist, we just create an empty list and return it:"

```
def load_orders(filename):
    if os.path.exists(filename):
        f = open(filename, "r")
        orders = json.load(f)
        return orders
    else:
        orders = []
        return orders
```

"Now the load function is ready!" he said and looked at Erik.

"I don't think I could write it myself," Erik said.

"Of course, it looks complicated when you do it the first time. But look, you can read it as if it was plain English, can't you?"

Erik looked at the function again and tried to read it. "If the file with `filename` exists, then open the file. Save it in the object called `f`. Then load the previous orders from that `f` file into `orders`. Hmmm, yes, I can read it." He was surprised. He could read Python now and understand it!

"The next function is easier," Simon continued. "I think you can write it yourself if you look at the file where you practiced with sample orders. Look, right after the two `append()` operations, there are three lines that we need here. We already have a function called `save_order()` that does nothing except print 'Saving order . . .'. Let's replace it with a real function. I think it should be called `save_orders()`—plural, because now we know how to save a list of orders in a JSON file, right?"

Simon wrote the beginning of the function:

```
def save_orders(orders, filename):
```

He explained, "We pass the list of orders as a first argument. Then we pass the name of the file where we want to store it. Now you can add those three lines from yesterday's program."

Erik looked at the `dict_json.py` file and copied three lines from it. Now the function looked like this:

```
def save_orders(orders, filename):
    f = open(filename, "w")
    json.dump(orders, f, indent=4)
    return
```

"Can we test it now?" he asked Simon.

"We're almost ready," Simon answered. "Look at the bottom of our file—we just call the `main_menu()` function. Here's what we have to do in this function," and he quickly drew a picture.

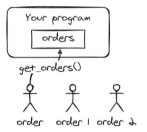

"This is what we do in the `main_menu()` function. We just have to edit it a little bit to serve several customers and save their orders in the `orders` list. We have to pass that list into the `main_menu()` function, where there is a place to save the orders as they are entered."

He moved the cursor to the beginning of the file and added the `orders` argument to the `main_menu()` definition:

```
def main_menu(orders):
```

"Now," he continued, "each time the customer enters a new order, it will be appended to the `orders` list. Before we added the list as an argument, `main_menu()` didn't know where to add the new order. Now we can use the `append()` method and add it to `orders` right after the customer confirms the order.

"We won't use the `save_order()` function here. We'll save all the orders when you close the program." Simon changed the `main_menu()` function to this:

```
def main_menu(orders):
    while True:
        order = get_order()
        print("Check your order:")
        print_order(order)
        confirm = input("Confirm? Press Y to confirm, N to cancel: ")
        if confirm == "Y" or confirm == "y":
            orders.append(order)          ⟵┐  Appends the new
            print("Thanks for your order:")  │  order to the list
            print_order(order)
        else:
            continue
```

"We'll also change the main program to perform three steps: load the previous orders, get the new orders (main menu), and save all the orders." Simon added those three lines to the bottom of the file, so it looked like this:

```
orders = load_orders("orders.json")
main_menu(orders)
save_orders(orders, "orders.json")
```

"Can I try it now?" Erik asked.

"Sure, go ahead!" Simon said.

Erik ran the program. He entered his name at the first prompt and then selected his drink components. When the program asked him to confirm the order, he typed Y. The program returned to the "What's your name:" prompt.

"Okay," Erik said, "it works. But how can I check my orders? Are they saved in the file?"

"Let's check," Simon said.

The brothers opened the orders.json file and were surprised to see that it still contained the old orders from yesterday's experiments—even Simon was confused.

"Let's see," he said. "We open the file, we read from it, we get the order . . . but we never write to the file because we're still in the main menu taking orders! We never reach that save_orders() function! Hmmm, let me think how to fix it."

Erik smiled. His know-it-all brother didn't know what to do. But that lasted only a moment.

Simon said, "I see. We didn't give the user a way to exit the main menu. We keep asking the user their name, but what if we want to end the program?"

"I saw that you pressed Control-C when you wanted to stop my program," Erik said.

"Yes, I did, but that's not a *normal* way of ending programs. When I did that, the program was *interrupted*. Usually, Python gives you an error message when you do that. When a program is interrupted, it doesn't do anything else—it just stops wherever it is. It won't write our orders to the file, and it won't close the file. Pressing Control-C is a bad way to end a program."

Simon paused for bit and then continued, "We should give the user a *normal* way of ending our program."

"Like Quit in the menu in Word?"

"Yes, like that. Let's tell the user that if they want to exit, they should enter X and only X when asked for their name. The probability that we'll have a customer whose real full name is 'X' is very low–almost zero, actually. So let's do this: if the customer enters the name X in the get_order() function, we won't ask any other questions and will return an empty order, like this: order = {}. This order then goes to the main_menu() function, and it decides what happens next: If the order is empty, it will save the order into the file and exit. If it's not empty, it will add the order to the list and continue working. Let's draw a diagram."

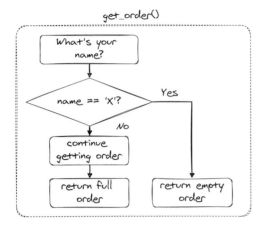

"This will be our updated `get_order()` function. Let me help you write it," Simon said. He took Erik's keyboard and started editing the `get_order()` function:

```
def get_order():
    order = {}
    name = input("Enter your name or enter 'X' to exit: ")
    if name == "X" or name == "x":        ◁─────┐  Checks both 'X' and 'x'
        return {}
    else:
        order["name"] = name
    drinks = read_menu("drinks.txt")
    flavors = read_menu("flavors.txt")
    toppings = read_menu("toppings.txt")
    order["drink"] = menu(drinks, "Erik's drinks",
                          "Choose your drink: ")
    order["flavor"] = menu(flavors, "Erik's flavors",
                           "Choose your flavor: ")
    order["topping"] = menu(toppings, "Erik's toppings",
                            "Choose your topping: ")
    return order
```

"In this function, I just followed the diagram we created together.

"Now for the main menu," Simon continued. "Here is another diagram." He started drawing.

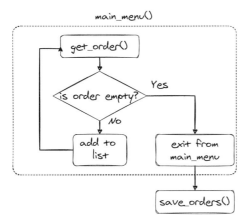

"As we discussed, if `get_order()` returns an empty order, we exit from the main menu. After that, our program saves the orders in the file." Simon edited the `main_menu()` function to the following:

```python
def main_menu(orders):
    while True:
        order = get_order()          # If the order is empty,
        if order == {}:              #  we have to exit.
            print("You entered 'X', exiting...")
            return
        print("Check your order:")
        print_order(order)
        confirm = input(
        "Confirm? Press Y to confirm, N to cancel, X to finish: ")
        if confirm == "Y" or confirm == "y":
            orders.append(order)
            print("Thanks for your order:")
            print_order(order)
        elif confirm == "X" or confirm == "x":
            return
        else:
            continue
```

> **Your Turn!   Edit the main menu function**
> Edit your main menu function like Simon did. If you need help, the full program code for this chapter is here: https://github.com/pavelanni/pythonicadventure-code/tree/main/ch09.

"And that's it," Simon said. "Let's test it. Just enter a different name this time, so you can easily see that it was added to the JSON file."

Erik started the program. He answered "Jason" when the program asked for his name. He entered the rest of his order and typed Y to confirm the order. The program asked for his name again.

"Now let's enter x and see if it exits properly," Simon suggested.

Erik typed x and pressed Enter.

`You entered 'x', exiting` . . . the program said. It then returned to the familiar >>> Python prompt.

"Now check the `orders.json` file," Simon said.

Erik started his text editor and opened the JSON file. Right at the bottom of the file, he found his recent order from 'Jason.'

"It worked!" he said. "It saved all the orders in the file, and now I can see them all!"

"Yes, you can," Simon said and smiled. He was happy to see a complete working program that took orders and stored them in the file. And it was written by his little brother!

"Congratulations, Erik!" Simon said. "I think now you can say that you created a real application. Look, it has input and output. It has data structures and algorithms. It checks for errors. It has data storage. And most importantly, it works and it's very useful—it collects orders. I'm absolutely serious—it's a good program. I'm very proud of you."

As usual, Simon drew a diagram. This time, it was of what he called a *real* program.

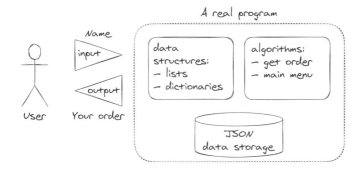

"Yes, I like my program too," Erik said. "It does what I want, and it looks good. It prints orders almost the same way I saw in Starbucks. Yes, almost . . . maybe I can add a couple of lines or stars to make it better. I have some other ideas about what to add to this program."

"What else do you want to add?" Simon asked.

"First of all, I want to make it a web application—with menus and buttons. It should be online, so I can take my iPad with me and use it."

"Great idea!" Simon said. "Let's start working on it next week. I have a couple of ideas too," he said and smiled.

"Why are you smiling?" Erik asked.

"I remembered how you thought you were done with the program after our first day."

"Ha, yes, I remember that too," Erik said. "Of course, the program wasn't quite ready then. What are your other ideas?"

Simon said, "I'd add a couple of things to our data structure. For example, we can add the date and time when the order was made. That way, we'll be able to see how many customers we served each day or each month."

"Yes, that would be good," Erik agreed.

"Then, maybe we should save orders in the data storage right after they are entered. That will make sure we keep all the previous orders even if the program fails and crashes."

"But you said it will make it slower," Erik remembered.

"Just a tiny bit. But it's worth it—otherwise, we risk losing all our orders. I'm thinking about using a database for that.

"Also," Simon continued, "we need functions like 'print all orders' and 'count how many portions of vanilla flavor we used' if we want to make your program a real business application."

"Of course, I want it," Erik said. "But first I want to make it a web application and make it beautiful."

"Sure, we can start working on that next week."

New things you have learned today

- *How to check if a file exists*—We used the `os` Python module and the `os.path.exists()` method to do this. You pass the filename, and it returns `True` or `False`.
- *Pressing Control-C is not a good way to end a program*—We use Control-C when we want to stop a program that behaves abnormally. Good programs should always give you a way to end them normally.
- *What a real program is*—We learned that real programs have input and output, data structures and algorithms, data storage, and error checking.

Code for this chapter

You can find the code for this chapter here: https://github.com/pavelanni/pythonicadventure-code/tree/main/ch09.

Learning Flask: Your first web application

"You said you wanted to create a web application?" Simon asked Erik the next week.

"Yes, sure!" Erik said. "Otherwise, how could I use my program on my iPad?"

"Okay, but be prepared: it's not an easy task. It will require all your attention. If you don't completely understand *everything* we do here, don't worry. I'll help you when you need it."

"I know—you're a good brother," Erik said. There was almost no irony in the way he said it.

"We'll use our good friend, the Mu editor, for our web application. It has a special mode for that. Start the editor and click Mode in the top-left corner."

Erik did and saw a menu.

"Scroll to the bottom," Simon said. "Find the Web mode and click it. Then click OK."

After Erik did that, Simon pointed to the bottom-right corner and said, "See this word 'Web' next to the cogwheel? That shows we've switched to Web mode. Now let's see what we can do with it—click New."

Erik did, and Python code immediately appeared in the editor window.

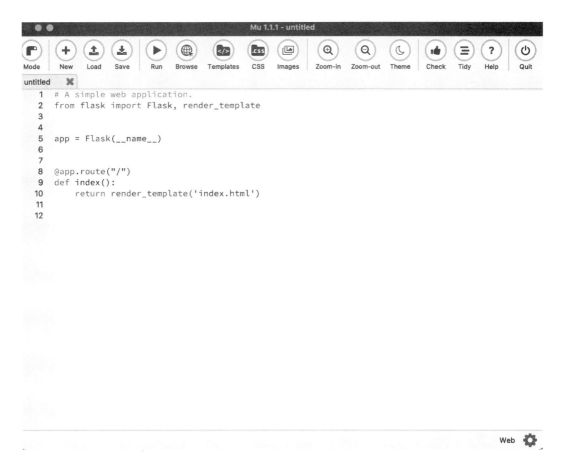

"Interesting," he said. "Mu already wrote something for me. Can I run it?"

"Sure, go ahead. First, you'll have to save it. Call it `first_app.py`."

Erik clicked Run and entered `first_app.py` in the Save dialog. He saw the output at the bottom of the window.

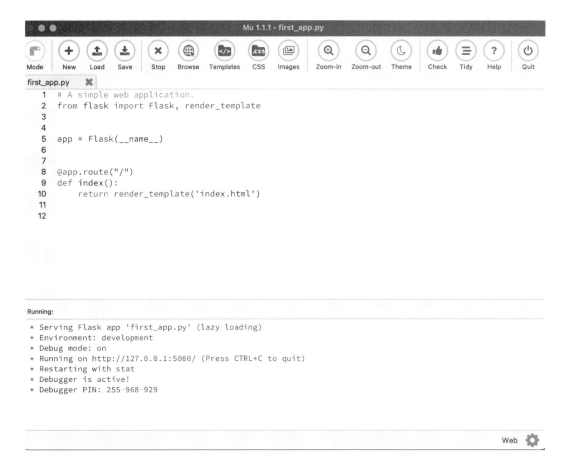

"What is that?" he asked.

"This tells you that your first web application is running. See this message: 'Running on http://127.0.0.1:5000/'? That means you can go to your browser and enter this address: http://127.0.0.1:5000/. Sometimes, this address is called a *URL* or *Uniform Resource Locator*—you'll hear those terms all the time when working with the web."

Erik opened a new tab in his browser and entered the address. He was surprised at what he saw.

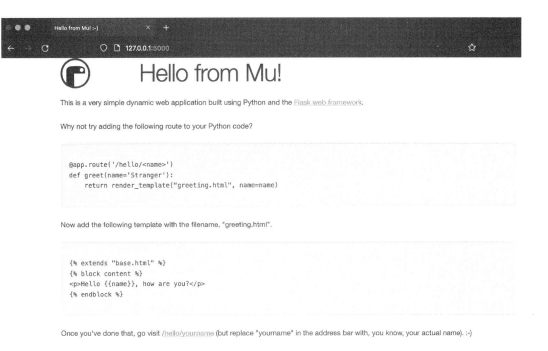

"Wait, is this all written by my editor?" he asked Simon.

"Yes, but look, Mu suggests that you write the rest yourself," Simon said. He pointed to the code example on the page. "Mu recommends you copy the code from the first gray window to your program. Go ahead and do that."

That was easy. Erik quickly copied the text and pasted it below the existing code.

"Now Mu tells you to create a new file," Simon continued. "Copy the text from the second window, and save it as a new file named greeting.html."

Erik knew how to do that. He clicked New in the Mu editor and removed the program Mu had put into it. He copied and pasted the text from the second gray window. Then he clicked Save.

Simon helped him, "Use the drop-down menu to change from '*.py' to 'Other (*.*)'. Otherwise, Mu will think you're trying to save a Python program. We need to tell it that this is a different type of file. In the Save As field, type greeting.html.

"Now stop the program and run it again," Simon said. "Don't forget to switch to the first_app.py tab."

Erik switched to the application tab, clicked Stop, and clicked Run again. He saw the same output at the bottom of the window.

"Now go back to your browser and do what it suggests. Look, it says 'Go visit /hello/yourname' and tells you to use your own name. Add `/hello/Erik` in the address bar, right after `5000`."

Now this looked like real hacking. Erik entered what Simon suggested and pressed Enter.

Hello!

Hello Erik, how are you?

"Wow! It talks to me!" He was really impressed.

"It's already *your* program that talks to you," Simon said. "That was easy, huh?"

"Wait," Erik said, "if we're going to work on this web stuff, I should call Emily. She told me she learned HTML, and this is what we need for the web, right?"

"Absolutely correct," Simon agreed. "Go ahead, call her. It's always good to work together."

***Your Turn!*   Create your first web application**
Switch to the Web mode in the Mu editor and create your first web application by copy-ing the example from the browser's page, just like Erik did. Try to run it with your name. Try other names. Show it to your friends and ask them to use their names.

Emily lived nearby. She arrived in about 15 minutes, very excited about the project. She said immediately, "Erik, show me your HTML!"

Erik showed her the `greeting.html` file. He said, "Well, it's not *my* code, it's from this Mu editor."
"Wow, interesting," Emily said. "I've never seen these curly braces in HTML."

"Right," Simon said, "because this isn't pure HTML—it's a *template*. We're using a program called Flask here, which is included with Mu, and it uses templates to gener-ate HTML."

"I see," Emily said. "But I know these `<h1>` and `<p>` tags."

"Tags? What are 'tags'?" Erik asked.

"Tags are these small pieces of code that you put in your text to change how it looks. Look here, you place `<h1>` before 'Hello!' and `</h1>` after it, and it looks larger. This is what in HTML is called a *header*, like chapter headers."

"What about `<p>`?" Erik asked.

"It means 'paragraph'," Emily explained. "In HTML, you can write your text how you want: in one long line, in many short lines, or one word per line. But if it has `<p>` at the beginning and `</p>` at the end, it will be displayed as one paragraph in the browser.

"There are a lot of other tags," she continued. "You can make your text bold or italic, change colors, and more."

"Emily, do you know anything about HTML forms?" Simon asked.

"They told us in class that we can create forms in HTML to enter text or use menus," Emily answered. "But I haven't tried them myself."

"Menus is what we want!" Erik exclaimed.

"I'll help you," Simon said. "First, we should use the mandatory HTML tags. We should always have `<html>` at the beginning of the file and `</html>` at the end. Also, we should use `<body>` tags around our text. Again, we use `<body>` to *open* the text and `</body>` to close it. That's why the tags with a slash, `/`, are called *closing* tags."

```
<html>
<body>

</body>
</html>
```

"Tags are like brackets in a list in Python," Erik said. He wanted to show Emily that he knew Python already.

"You're right," Simon confirmed. "These tags *enclose* some text and explain its meaning. Some pieces of text are headers, some are paragraphs. But now we want to create a menu. For that, we'll need a `<form>` tag first and then a `<select>` tag inside it. Let's create a very simple menu." He started writing.

Listing 10.1   The first menu form with two options

```
<html>
<body>
<form>
    <select>
      <option>Coffee</option>
      <option>Decaf</option>
    </select>
    <input type="submit" value="Submit">
</form>
</body>
</html>
```

> **Your Turn!   Create your first web form**
>
> Create a `forms.html` file and save it under `mu_code/templates`. Copy the preceding code and test it in your browser. Try to change the options and add more options.

Simon finished writing and clicked Save. He saved the file as `forms.html` under the `mu_code/templates` directory. "How many elements enclosed in tags do you see here? Emily, you should be more familiar with that."

Emily started counting. "First, the `<html>` tag, then the `<body>` tag. Inside the body we have a `<form>`, and inside the form we have `<select>`. It's for the menu, correct? And then in the select, we have two `<option>` elements."

"Right. You did a great job, Emily," Simon said. "And don't forget the `<input>` element, which is a part of the form. It doesn't have a closing tag—it exists by itself. We use it to create the Submit button."

"Let's see what it looks like in the browser," Simon continued.

"Can you open *files* in the browser?" Erik asked. "I thought browsers are only for websites."

"Of course, you can," Emily answered. "We did it all the time in our HTML class! You just use the File menu in your browser and then click Open File. Then you find your file. That's it."

Erik did what Emily just said and opened the `forms.html` file. He saw a menu, very similar to what he had seen and used on many sites. He clicked the menu, and it opened.

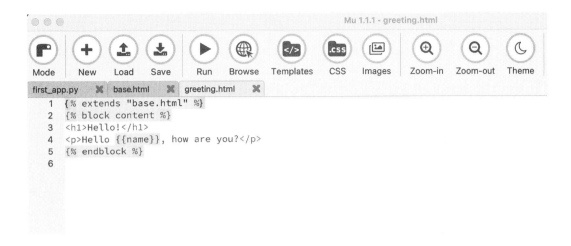

"I didn't know that you could create forms so easily," Emily said.

"Yes, it's pretty easy to create a simple form like this, but there are some missing parts," Simon said.

"It looks good to me," Erik said. "What's missing?"

"Yes, it *looks* good, but it doesn't *do* anything," Simon said. "We have to get data from the user and then *pass* that data to the program. How can we pass the data?" Simon asked. He then answered his own question, "We should use variables and values, very similar to Python. Let me add something to this form:

Listing 10.2   The updated form with a variable and the `action` target

```
<html>
<body>
<form action="/order" method="post">
    <select name="drink">     </select>
    <input type="submit" value="Submit">
      <option value="">- Choose drink -</option>
      <option value="coffee">Coffee</option>
      <option value="decaf">Decaf</option>
</form>
</body>
</html>
```

Defines the variable the menu will return

Adds an option that tells the user what to do

Defines the values the menu options will return

"First," Simon said, "we define the *variable* we want to return from this menu. In this menu, the variable is called `drink`.

"In the first option, we tell the user what to do. This option will show first in the menu and work as a prompt. As you can see, its value is empty. If the user hasn't chosen a drink, they will see this prompt. You can't prepare their order without this information, can you?

"Finally, the next two options define the *value* this menu option can return. It's similar to what we did when we chose items from a text menu, remember?"

"Can I try it?" Erik asked.

"Of course, go ahead and open the file again. Or just reload it in the browser."

Erik reloaded the file and chose Decaf from the menu. Then he clicked Submit.

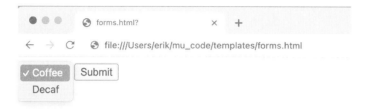

"What's that?" he asked, visibly puzzled.

"Oh, I forgot to tell you," Simon said. "Look, I changed the `form` tag a little bit.

Listing 10.3   The `action` target

```
<form action="/order" method="post">
```

"Each form should have an *action*," he started to explain. "An action is something that our application will do when the user submits the form. When the user makes their choice—coffee or decaf—they should *pass* this information to some function. That function should know what to do with this information: store it in the file or database, print the order, and so on."

"Like what we did in our previous program?" Erik asked.

"You keep talking about your 'previous' program. Can you show it to me?" Emily demanded.

"I'm sorry, Emily," Simon said. "I should have explained it earlier. I worked with Erik on a program that collects orders in a coffee shop, similar to Starbucks, where you can order a drink, add flavors and toppings, and all that. Erik wrote a program that shows menus and asks the customer what they want to order. When they choose their drinks, flavors, and toppings, the program prints the order. But the program only works in a terminal, in text mode, for now. Erik needs your help to convert it to a web application."

"This sounds like a cool project!" Emily said. "I hope Erik will teach me Python too."

"Of course," Simon said. "Teaching somebody is the best way to learn.

"Back to our form," he continued. "That `action` attribute tells the browser: 'After the user submits the form, open this address and pass the information from the form there.' In our case, the address is called `/order`.

"Don't worry, it only sounds scary—I'll show you what to do with it," Simon added. He noticed the confusion on Emily's and Erik's face.

"I still don't understand," Erik said. "Where is this address that you're talking about?"

"Look at your first application," Simon said. "See this `greet` function? This function was written by the Mu editor for us—or, rather, by its authors," Simon said. "You see the now familiar function definition that starts with `def`, but, right above it, you can see something new: `@app.route('/hello/<name>')`. In Python, it's called a *decorator*, but we aren't going to learn about decorators today.

```
@app.route('/hello/<name>')
def greet(name='Stranger'):
    return render_template("greeting.html", name=name)
```

"What's important for us today is that you can use it to tell your program which function to use for which address."

"Aha, the address is that `/hello/Erik` I entered in the browser! I see now," Erik said. "Let's show Emily how it works." He opened the tab with the `first_app.py` file in the editor and clicked Run. Then he clicked Browse. His browser opened a page with greetings from Mu.

"Emily, look, I can type the address here, right after these numbers, `127.0.0.1:5000`. Look what it shows us!" Erik typed `/hello/Emily` and pressed Enter. The browser showed them the result.

Your file couldn't be accessed

It may have been moved, edited, or deleted.

ERR_FILE_NOT_FOUND

"Wow, I like it!" Emily said. "Can I try?" She changed "Emily" to "Erik". Of course, the browser showed the page with "Hello Erik, how are you?"

"Interesting!" she said. "In our HTML class, we could change pages, but we had to edit HTML. This is much easier!"

"Right," Simon said. "This is what we call *dynamic* pages—pages that change depending on what you enter. You can enter your information in the address, like `/hello/Emily`, or you can use forms. Then the page is *generated* using the information you entered. I'm sure you've seen this kind of page many times—for example, when you enter a comment or chat with someone on the web. You click Submit or just press Enter, and the page is updated, right? Now you'll learn how to make such pages yourself.

"Let me show it in a diagram," he said. Simon started drawing.

"This combination of letters and numbers at the top of your browser is the *address* or *URL*. I labeled it in blue. Usually, you'll see the site's name here, like `google.com`. In our case, it uses numbers, which are the site's IP address. We're using your own computer, and, for every computer in the world, the address `127.0.0.1` means 'this computer.' But don't worry about that now."

Simon pointed to the first red circle around the word 'order' in the address and said, "This is what you should care about. Look, it's part of the address. When we open this address, we see the form with the drinks menu. When you click Submit," and he followed the arrow down his diagram, "the form knows that it should find the function responsible for the `/order` address. You see, it's here, in the `form action` field.

"And then," he followed the arrow up to the Python block, "the form finds the Python function that can work with it, because we used the `@app.route('/order')` decorator. You see, these three things are connected; you just have to use the same name in the address, form, and Python program."

"I see that the function is also called 'order'—is that the fourth place where we use it?" Erik asked.

"You have a very sharp eye!" Simon said and smiled. "No, in this case, the function can have a different name. I could call it 'new_order' or 'get_order'.

"But now we have to write the actual function. I'll help you here. It will look a bit scary, but don't worry. I'm learning this Flask system myself, and, usually, I follow the online tutorial and take examples from there. Don't think that I remember all these things myself."

Simon wrote the function, looking at the example he kept open in the browser. "In the first line, you see the words GET and POST. These are the *methods* that we use with web servers. We use GET when we want to get something from a web server, like a web page. We use POST to *send* information to the web server. Like in this case—we want to send or POST the drink chosen by the customer. To put it another way: when you load a page in the browser, you use GET; and when you click Submit in your form, you use POST. You'll understand it better when we start using it, don't worry.

"Below that, we start using one of the words, POST: `if request.method == 'POST':`. Look at what it says: if the method is POST, which means somebody filled out the form and clicked Submit, we read the information they entered in the form and print it.

"Remember that we used `<select name="drink">` in the form? This is the name we use in the next line, in the square brackets: `drink = request.form['drink']`. Later, we'll add other menus for flavors and toppings. In the form, they will have names like `flavor` and `topping`. Here, in the code, we'll use them as `request.form['flavor']` and `request.form['topping']`.

"In the `print` line, we just print whatever we received from the form. You'll see it in the editor.

"In the last line, we tell our web server to print this page with the menu. It's like the menu loop that we used in our program before—you get the information from the customer, print it out, and return to the menu to get another order. You repeat this loop until you're done entering orders."

The following listing shows the function Simon wrote:

Listing 10.4   The function to process an order

```
@app.route('/order', methods=('GET', 'POST'))    ⟵── Methods that we'll use with this form
def order():
    if request.method == 'POST':    ⟵── The POST method means we're submitting information.
        drink = request.form['drink']    ⟵┐
        print("Drink: ", drink)    ⟵┐    │
                                                Gets the customer choice from
                                                the form's field called drink
  ┌─▷ return render_template("forms.html")
  │                                          Prints the choice we've received
  │ Display the forms.html template.
```

"Let me add one more thing," Simon said. He added `request` to the first line with `import`. "This module, called `request`, is a part of Flask. If we use it, we have to import it." Now the first line looked like this:

```
from flask import Flask, render_template, request
```

> ***Your Turn!*   Write your own `order()` function**
>
> Add the preceding `order()` function to your `first_app.py` program. Don't forget to change the `import` line.
>
> Then try to run it. Open a new tab in the browser and use the `http://127.0.0.1:5000/order` address. If you're having problems, continue reading and follow what Emily and Erik are doing.

"Can I run it now?" Erik asked. He was a bit tired after such a long explanation. Emily, on the other hand, listened to Simon's explanations as if he was a wizard. She liked all this programming magic and couldn't wait to try the program.

"Can I run it?" Emily asked.

"Of course," Erik said. "Just click Save and then Run."

"Now click Browse," Simon said.

Emily did, and the page opened in a new browser tab.

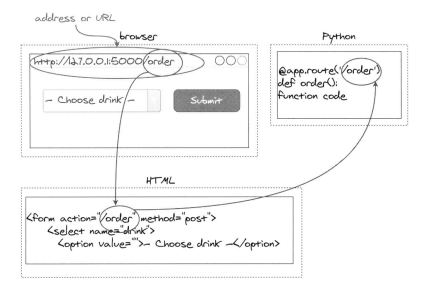

"Now we have to add /order to the address, remember?" Simon helped her.

Emily did, and the address line in the browser became: `http://127.0.0.1:5000/order`. The page showed the menu they just created together.

"Go ahead. Choose your drink and click Submit," Simon said.

Emily chose Decaf and clicked Submit. She got the same page with the Choose Drink menu.

"Did it work?" she asked. She looked confused.

"Let's check," Simon said. "Go back to the editor. Look at the bottom window."

"Do you see this line: `Drink:  decaf`? It's what our program is printing," Simon said. "That means it works!"

"But I thought that it would print the order on the page," Emily said.

"It will, trust me," Simon said. "We haven't written that part yet. We're getting there, right now."

He took the keyboard and changed the `first_app.py` file by adding one line after the `print()` line. Simon explained, "When we first open the `/order` address in the browser, that means we use the GET method. We want to *get* the page first, right? We don't have anything to POST yet. In that case, we use the `forms.html` template that displays our drink menu.

"But after we have chosen a drink and clicked Submit, we use the POST method. We want to *send* this information to the program. In that case, we collect the data from the form—the drink choice—and we use *another* template. I called it `print.html`, because we want to print the order."

The `order()` function now looked like this:

```
@app.route('/order', methods=('GET', 'POST'))
def order():
    if request.method == 'POST':
        drink = request.form['drink']
        print("Drink: ", drink)
        return render_template("print.html", drink=drink)   ⟵  Prints the order using
                                                                the print.html template

    return render_template("forms.html")
```

"But we don't have a file called `print.html`," Emily said.

"Right, I'm going to create it right now." Simon created another file in the editor and saved it as `print.html` under `templates`:

Listing 10.5 A template to print the order (first version)

```
{% extends "base.html" %}
{% block content %}
<h1>Thanks for your order!</h1>
<p>Your drink: <strong>{{drink}}</strong></p>
{% endblock %}
```

Emily looked at his code and said, "Oh, this I can understand! You print the header, 'Thanks for your order', and then you open a new paragraph and print 'Your drink', and then in bold you print the drink itself. And this drink in double curly braces works the same way it worked with my name when it printed 'Hello Emily', right?"

"Exactly right!" exclaimed Simon. "You're absolutely correct, Emily!"

> **Your Turn!   Edit your web form to print the drink choice on the page**
> Copy the preceding template into your print.html file. Feel free to change the title and the text. Change the first_app.py file by adding the line with return and save it too. Try running your program.

"Can I try it?" Emily asked.

"Sure, go ahead and click Run," Simon said.

Emily clicked Run and chose Coffee from the menu. She saw the updated page.

```
Running:
127.0.0.1 - - [16/Oct/2022 12:22:56] " [36mGET /static/img/logo.png HTTP/1.1 [0m" 304 -
127.0.0.1 - - [16/Oct/2022 12:27:22] "GET /order HTTP/1.1" 200 -
127.0.0.1 - - [16/Oct/2022 12:27:22] " [36mGET /static/css/normalize.css HTTP/1.1 [0m" 304 -
127.0.0.1 - - [16/Oct/2022 12:27:22] " [36mGET /static/css/skeleton.css HTTP/1.1 [0m" 304 -
Drink:  decaf
127.0.0.1 - - [16/Oct/2022 12:30:23] "POST /order HTTP/1.1" 200 -
127.0.0.1 - - [16/Oct/2022 12:30:23] " [36mGET /static/css/normalize.css HTTP/1.1 [0m" 304 -
127.0.0.1 - - [16/Oct/2022 12:30:23] " [36mGET /static/css/skeleton.css HTTP/1.1 [0m" 304 -
```

"Yeah, it works!" she exclaimed.

"It's like calling the print_order() function in our previous program," Erik said.

"Yes, exactly!" Simon said.

"But how do I get back to the order page?" Erik asked.

"You see that the address in the browser is still pointing to /order?" Simon asked. "That means if you click the address line with the mouse and press Enter, you'll reload the order page. Just don't click the reload button, or it will create another order."

Emily did what Simon said, and she saw the order page again.

"But there is a better way," Simon said. "You were looking for a button on the print page, like Back To The Order Page, weren't you?"

"Yes, that would be easier," Emily agreed.

"We can use another form for that," Simon said. "It will be very simple." He added several lines to the `templates/print.html` file.

"Look, I created another form that has only the Submit button. I just renamed it to 'New order'. Look, it points to `/order` in its `action` field. That means when we click the New Order button, it will send us to the `/order` page, and it will show the drink menu again. Try it!"

Listing 10.6   The updated print template with the New Order button

```
{% extends "base.html" %}
{% block content %}
<h1>Thanks for your order!</h1>
<p>Your drink: <strong>{{drink}}</strong></p>

<form action="/order">
<input type="submit" value="New order" />
</form>
{% endblock %}
```

Emily did, and, after she clicked Submit, she saw a page with the new button.

She clicked the button and got back to the order page.

Erik noted, "It's like our main menu with a loop. Order, then confirm, then print, and then back to the order menu."

"You're right!" Simon confirmed. "Let me show it in a diagram.

"Look at the diagram. Step one: you choose Decaf from the menu. This assigns the value `decaf` to the `drink` variable in the form.

"Step two: that value `decaf` is passed to our Python program via `request.form`. Now the `drink` variable in the Python program has the value `decaf`.

"Step three: we pass the value of the `drink` variable from Python—which is `decaf`—to the `drink` variable in the `print.html` template.

"Step four: we call `render_template()` with the `drink` variable, which is replaced with its value, `decaf`. And now `decaf` is printed on the web page.

"Finally, step five: we click New Order and return to the order page.

> **Your Turn!   Change the `print.html` template**
> Add a New Order button to the `templates/print.html` template. Test it. Can you return to the order page?

"Emily and Erik, you did a great job today," Simon said. "Most importantly, you didn't fall asleep during all those long explanations."

"I almost did," Erik said.

"Yes, I noticed," Simon said and smiled. "But seriously, creating web applications is 10 times more difficult than working on text menus and dialogues. I admire your patience!"

"But it was worth it," Emily said. "The program works now!"

"We also need to add flavors and toppings," Erik said.

"Right!" Simon said. "We have to create all the menus, but in the web form. I'm pretty sure Emily will help you with that."

"Sure," Emily said. "It looks like we need to add more `select` forms to the template. Erik, will you show me your previous program? We can start working on the web application tomorrow."

"Of course," Erik said. "Let's get together tomorrow and work on that."

"I'll be happy to help," Simon said. "Please let me know when you start."

New things you have learned today

- *Web mode in Mu editor*—In addition to the standard Python mode, the Mu editor also has a web mode. It has a simple web application example.
- *HTML forms*—This is a way to get information from users into a web application. You can have menus, text fields, and buttons. When you click Submit, the form sends information to a special address configured in the `action` field. From that address, the information can be processed by a program.
- *Flask*—A program that helps us create web applications. It's being developed by the open source community, and it has good tutorials and examples. It's used by many online sites and web applications.

Code for this chapter

You can find the code for this chapter here: https://github.com/pavelanni/pythonicadventure-code/tree/main/ch10.

Web form for orders:
Coffee shop on the web

11

In this chapter

- Emily and Erik create a real web form for their shop
- Simon explains how to pass values from the form to the program
- Erik and Emily learn about form elements, such as `input` and `select`
- Simon explains how files work

The next day, Erik, Emily, and Simon got together to continue working on the Coffee Shop application.

"Are you ready to get serious?" Simon asked. "Today, we have to work on our *actual* web form. We tried a very simple menu yesterday. Now we have to add two more menus and the text field where the customer can enter their name.

"Let's look at our code from yesterday. We already created one menu there—the code between the `<select>` and `</select>` tags. This menu already has two options: coffee and decaf.

Listing 11.1   First menu options in `templates/forms.html`

```
{% extends "base.html" %}
{% block content %}

<form action="/order" method="post">
    <select name="drink">
        <option value="">- Choose drink -</option>
        <option value="coffee">Coffee</option>      ◁──┐  Menu option for coffee
        <option value="decaf">Decaf</option>    ◁──┐
    </select>                                    │  Menu option for decaf
    <input type="submit" value="Submit">
</form>
{% endblock %}
```

"Now we have to add another option to the `drink` menu. Erik, I think you had 'chocolate' in that menu, right?"

"Yes, coffee, chocolate, and decaf," Erik confirmed.

"Good. And what about flavors and toppings?"

"For flavors, we have caramel, vanilla, peppermint, raspberry, and plain," Erik said. "For toppings, we have chocolate, cinnamon, and caramel."

"Yummy," Emily said.

"Here is a task for you," Simon said. "First, add the third option to the `drink` menu. Second, add two more menus for flavors and toppings. It will require some copying, pasting, and typing—and attention too. Who's at the keyboard?"

"I am," Emily said. "I can do it. I'm familiar with HTML and all these tags."

"Very well, go ahead!"

Emily started editing the file. Erik was watching and asking questions from time to time.

"Why did you move the `<option>` line to the right? Does HTML have the same rules about indentation as Python?"

"No, in HTML you don't have to indent lines," Emily answered. "I could write them all from the first position, but this looks better. In my class, our teacher said it's good for *readability*."

"Yes, Simon told me the same," Erik said. "In Python, you *have* to use indentation for blocks, but in some cases you're free to choose whether to put your code on one line or use new lines and indentation. Simon said you should write *readable* code—at least for yourself."

With Erik's help, Emily listed all the options for flavors and toppings and created the following HTML template:

Listing 11.2   Additional menu options in `templates/forms.html`

```
{% extends "base.html" %}
{% block content %}

<form action="/order" method="post">
```

```
    <select name="drink">
      <option value="">- Choose drink -</option>
      <option value="coffee">Coffee</option>
      <option value="chocolate">Chocolate</option>
      <option value="decaf">Decaf</option>
    </select>
    <select name="flavor">
      <option value="">- Choose flavor -</option>
      <option value="caramel">Caramel</option>
      <option value="vanilla">Vanilla</option>
      <option value="peppermint">Peppermint</option>
      <option value="raspberry">Raspberry</option>
      <option value="plain">Plain</option>
    </select>
    <select name="topping">
      <option value="">- Choose topping -</option>
      <option value="chocolate">Chocolate</option>
      <option value="cinnamon">Cinnamon</option>
      <option value="caramel">Caramel</option>
    </select>

    <input type="submit" value="Submit">
</form>

{% endblock %}
```

> **Your Turn!   Create your menus**
> Create the new menus in the `templates/forms.html` file. Feel free to use different options. Take some ideas from your local coffee or ice cream shop.

Simon looked at their code and said, "Looks good to me. But before we switch from HTML to Python, let's add one more thing to the form. Remember, we also asked the customer's name."

"Like in Starbucks!" Emily said.

"Exactly," Simon said. "Let me add one more line to your form. It's called `input`, and it has a type of `text`. We'll use it to enter the name. You see, I added it right after the `form` line.

Listing 11.3   Text field to enter a name in `templates/forms.html`

```
{% extends "base.html" %}
{% block content %}

<form action="/order" method="post">
    <input type="text" name="name" placeholder="ENTER NAME">
    <select name="drink">
      <option value="">- Choose drink -</option>
      <option value="coffee">Coffee</option>
. . .
```

> ### Your Turn! Add an `input` field
> Add an `input` field for the customer's name. Don't forget to put a placeholder as a hint for the user.

"Take a look at the HTML code again," Simon continued. "All three menus that Emily added, and the `input` line, are between the opening `<form>` tag and the closing `</form>` tag. Emily did a great job of indenting them for readability.

"Now we can clearly see that they are inside the form. That means they all are parts of the *same form*. So, when you click Submit, they will all be passed to the program together.

"In the program, we'll be able to read them using the `request.form` dictionary, exactly as we did in our simple program."

"As in `request.form['drink']`?" Erik asked.

"Yes, right," Simon answered. "Look, Emily gave them names, `flavor` and `topping`, so we can use those as keys for the dictionary in our program. Let's open our `first_app.py` again and see where we have to make changes. Remember what we do here? We get the form dictionary and copy the value for the `drink` key to the `drink` variable. For example, if the customer chooses `chocolate`, it will be assigned to the `drink` variable. That variable will be passed to the form called `print.html` to be displayed—or, some say *rendered*—on the page."

Listing 11.4 First version of `order()` in `first_app.py`

```
. . . .
@app.route("/order", methods=("GET", "POST"))
def order():
    if request.method == "POST":
        drink = request.form["drink"]
        print("Drink: ", drink)
        return render_template("print.html", drink=drink)

    return render_template("forms.html")
```

Simon continued, "Now that we're getting more values from the form, we should collect them all and pass them to the template. Can you add those lines, Erik?"

"I think so," Erik said.

Erik had added lines for flavor and topping when Simon said, "Don't forget about the `name`!"

Erik added it, and his code now looked like this:

Listing 11.5 More menu options passed to the print template in `first_app.py`

```
. . . .
@app.route("/order", methods=("GET", "POST"))
def order():
    if request.method == "POST":
        name=request.form["name"]
```

```
        drink=request.form["drink"]
        flavor=request.form["flavor"]
        topping=request.form["topping"]
        return render_template("print.html",
            name=name,
            drink=drink,
            flavor=flavor,
            topping=topping)

    return render_template("forms.html")
```

> ### *Your Turn!*   **Edit your Flask application**
> Edit your `first_app.py` program and add the variables like Erik did. Don't run it yet, because you don't have the `print.html` file.

"Great job, Erik!" Simon said. "Well, maybe it's too early to say that before we test it," and he smiled.

"Now there's just one small thing left," Simon continued. "We have to add these variables to the `print.html` template. Let's open it in the editor. Look, in addition to the main drink, we have to print the flavor and the topping. Oh, and don't forget that we now know the customer's name. It would be polite to print a greeting. Emily, can you edit this HTML?"

"Of course," Emily said. She started editing, explaining it to Erik while doing it.

"First, let's replace 'Thanks for your order' with 'Hello' and the name of the customer. I'm leaving it here as <h1> to make it bold and big.

"Then we'll put 'Here is your order' in <h2>," she continued. "It will be a bit smaller. After that, we'll print the order: main drink, flavor, and topping, each in a separate paragraph. I'll keep using the <strong> tag to print it in bold. At the bottom of the page, we have a simple form with only one button to get us back to the order page. I hope you remember it from yesterday."

Listing 11.6   Template to print the order in `templates/print.html`

```
{% extends "base.html" %}
{% block content %}

<h1>Hello {{name}}!</h1>

<h2>Here is your order:</h2>

<p>Drink: <strong>{{drink}}</strong></p>
<p>Flavor: <strong>{{flavor}}</strong></p>
<p>Topping: <strong>{{topping}}</strong></p>

<form action="/order">
<input type="submit" value="New order" />        This form, with a single button,
</form>                                           gets us back to the order page.
{% endblock %}
```

> ### Your Turn! Create a `templates/print.html` template
>
> Create a template for printing as Emily just did. Pay attention to the variables: you should use the variables that you passed from the program. If you changed the `first_app.py` file and used different variables, change them here too. Then try running the application.

"Can we try it now?" Erik asked.

"Have you saved all your files?" Simon asked. "Look at your tabs in the editor. Mu shows them with a small red circle if you haven't saved them."

"Everything is fine," Erik said.

"Then switch to the Python tab and click Run."

Erik did so and then clicked Browse. His browser opened a new tab with the familiar "Hello from Mu!" page. Erik added `/order` to the address line, and he saw the menu.

"Let me try it!" Emily said. She entered her name and chose Chocolate, Vanilla, and Caramel. She clicked Submit and got her order printed.

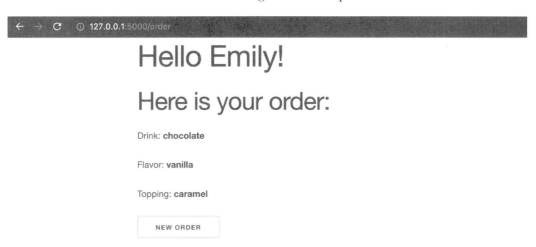

"Wow, it works!" She was excited to see a real web application they just wrote together.

"This is great," Simon said. "Now we have to add the functions we wrote for the text version."

"What functions?" Emily was puzzled. She thought it was done already. "Erik, can you explain?"

"What we have written here," he started, "is a user interface for our application. We did this before, but in a text mode. This web application looks so much better. But in addition to printing the order, we also want to save it in a file. We may want to count how many orders we served with caramel, for example."

"I see, to know when to buy more caramel for the shop," Emily said.

"Exactly! You think like a shop manager, Emily!" Simon said.

He continued, "Just before you joined us, we created a function to save the orders in a file. Our program saved the orders when we told it we were finished. The next time we started the program, it loaded all the previous orders into a list and was ready to add new orders to it."

Simon stopped for a while, thinking. "But with this new web application, we'll have to do it slightly differently."

"Why?" Erik asked.

"Because our application is running all the time, and we're not going to stop it. This kind of application is called a *web service*. It doesn't stop. It runs all the time. Even more, if something happens to it and it crashes for some reason, another program restarts it to make sure it's always ready to respond to requests— in our case, to accept orders."

"For us," Simon continued, "it means that we have to save each order right after we receive it. Let me quickly find the right way of doing that."

He opened a new tab in the browser and searched for a couple of minutes. "I know now," he said finally. "Erik, let's open our previous program and copy the `load_orders ()` and `save_orders()` functions into our web application."

"Where are we going to use them? In the `order()` function?" he asked Simon. "You told me last time that I should have them in the code *before* I use them, right?"

"Yes, absolutely right," Simon said. "Place them at the very beginning, even before the `app = Flask(name)` line. That way, we'll separate our file functions from the web application functions. Also, don't forget to add `import json` and `import os`."

Erik copied the functions from the `main_menu.py` file they had worked on several days ago.

Simon checked his work and said, "Good. We just have to close the file after we load the orders and, most importantly, after we save them."

"But we didn't do that before. Why should we do it now? And what does *close the file* mean exactly?" Erik asked.

Simon said, "We talked about that some time ago. Let me find the diagram. Emily, I think you'll want to know it too."

"Is it something like closing a file in Word?" Emily asked.

"Yes, but, in this case, we should do it from our Python program. It's important to understand that, until you close the file, Python keeps the orders in memory. If something happens to our computer and it shuts down, all the orders would be lost. So, we have to close the file to make sure the orders are all saved to the drive. Look at the diagram.

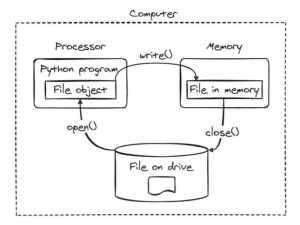

Your Turn!   Try to explain how files work

Use this diagram and try to explain to somebody else how files work. Do you understand it better after you have explained it?

"We didn't do this before, because our program automatically closed all the files when we ended it. In this web application, we're going to close the file with the orders every time we get a new order."

"But you said that slows down the program," Erik said.

"Yes, it does a little bit. But engineering is all about tradeoffs—this is what my robotics teacher keeps telling us. Our program is becoming more realistic, so we should think about saving important data—even if it makes the program a bit slower."

Simon added the `f.close()` method in both functions, so the functions now looked like the following listing:

Listing 11.7   Functions to load and save orders in `first_app.py`

```python
import os
import json

from flask import Flask, render_template, request

def save_orders(orders, filename):
    f = open(filename, "w")
    json.dump(orders, f, indent=4)
    f.close()
    return

def load_orders(filename):
    if os.path.exists(filename):
        f = open(filename, "r")
        orders = json.load(f)
```

```
        f.close()
        return orders
    else:
        orders = []
        return orders
```

. . . .

Simon added, "Of course, it would be better to use a database here. Maybe we'll add that later.

"Now we have to load the orders from the file," Simon said. He added a line just before the `Flask` line:

```
. . . .
orders = load_orders("orders.json")

app = Flask(name)
. . . .
```

"Now we have a list of orders to which we'll add new orders. That gives me an idea." Simon started typing, explaining himself while doing it.

"We have a list where we keep orders, and it's a list of Python dictionaries, right? So, when we get the new order from the form, we'd better copy it to a dictionary, not to separate variables. We'll append that dictionary to the list and then save it to the file. Even better, we can pass the dictionary to the HTML template to display it. That will simplify our program!"

He finished typing, and the `order()` function now looked like this:

```
@app.route("/order", methods=("GET", "POST"))
def order():
    if request.method == "POST":
        new_order = {"name": request.form["name"],
                     "drink": request.form["drink"],
                     "flavor": request.form["flavor"],
                     "topping": request.form["topping"]
                     }
        orders.append(new_order)
        save_orders(orders, "orders.json")
        return render_template(
            "print.html", new_order=new_order
        )

    return render_template("forms.html")
```

Appends the new order to the list

Creates a new dictionary from the form

Saves the list in the JSON file

Passes the dictionary to the template

> ### *Your Turn!* **Edit the application**
> Use the three previous listings and edit your `first_app.py` program. Make sure you understand what's happening when you create a new order and pass it to the template.

"Finally, we need to change the HTML template," Simon said. "Emily, would you help me?"

"Sure, but I don't know what to do," she answered.

"Look, we used to pass variables to the template to display them on the page: `name`, `flavor`, and so on. Now, instead of four variables, we'll pass just one—the `new_order` dictionary—that contains all four. It's called a *dictionary* in Python. You give it a key, and it returns the value. For example, you give it `flavor`, and it returns `caramel`."

"Yes, Erik explained about dictionaries in Python already. But how can we use them in HTML?"

"Exactly the same way as we do in Python: with square brackets! Let me show you," Simon said. He replaced `name` with `new_order["name"]` in the `Hello` line.

"I see it now," Emily said. She started changing the other variables. The following listing shows the `print.html` template after she finished:

Listing 11.10 Using a dictionary in `templates/print.html`

```
{% extends "base.html" %}
{% block content %}

<h1>Hello {{new_order["name"] }}!</h1>

<h2>Here is your order:</h2>

<p>Drink: <strong>{{ new_order["drink"] }}</strong></p>
<p>Flavor: <strong>{{ new_order["flavor"] }}</strong></p>
<p>Topping: <strong>{{ new_order["topping"] }}</strong></p>

<form action="/order">
<input type="submit" value="New order" />
</form>
{% endblock %}
```

> ### *Your Turn!* **Edit the `templates/print.html` file**
> Edit your print template and change from using variables to using the dictionary. Pay attention to the dictionary keys—if you changed them in the Python program, you should change them here. Try running the application now.

"Great!" Simon said. "Ready to test it?"

"Yes!" Erik said. He opened the usual address, `http://127.0.0.1/order`.

He entered `Alex` and chose `chocolate`, `vanilla`, and `cinnamon`. He got the order.

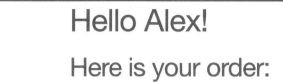

Hello Alex!

Here is your order:

Drink: **chocolate**

Flavor: **vanilla**

Topping: **cinnamon**

```
NEW ORDER
```

"Now we have to check if it saved this order to the file," Simon said.

He found the `orders.json` file in the `mu_code` folder and opened it with a text editor. "Yes!" he said. "Our program saved it in the file! Look—the first order is from the day when we tested the `save_order()` function. But the second order is what you just added. Very good!"

```
⬤ ⬤ ⬤                          📄 orders.json
[
  {
      "name": "Erik",
      "drink": "coffee",
      "flavor": "caramel",
      "topping": "chocolate"
  },
  {
      "name": "Alex",
      "drink": "chocolate",
      "flavor": "vanilla",
      "topping": "cinnamon"
  }
]
```

"But what about the menu files?" Erik asked.

"What menu files?"

"Remember," Erik explained, "you told me that the shop manager might not know Python. So, we created our menus in plain text files. Now our menu is in HTML, but I think the shop manager might not know HTML either. Can we do the same with this web application and let the shop manager edit text files instead of HTML if they want to add something to the menu?"

"Great idea, Erik!" Simon answered. "I think it's possible with HTML templates, but I'll have to check the Flask documentation. But, before you go, let's quickly recap what we learned today."

"You explained how files work in a computer. I didn't know that before," Erik said.

"I learned about the `input` field in HTML forms," Emily said. "And it was great to work on a real application, not on exercises for the class."

"I agree," Simon said. "I think the best way to learn something is to work on a real project. We've done a lot today, so let's take a rest and start working on Erik's idea tomorrow."

New things you have learned today

- *Web service*—A web service is a program that runs constantly and responds to requests, like a new order in the coffee shop.
- *Why it's important to close files*—When you work with files, Python keeps the updates in memory. If you want to make sure your data is saved on a permanent drive, you should call `f.close()`.

Code for this chapter

You can find the code for this chapter here: https://github.com/pavelanni/pythonicadventure-code/tree/main/ch11.

Database:
We need good storage

12

In this chapter

- Simon proposes a separate folder for the application
- Erik and Emily move the application files to the new folder structure
- Erik reuses the functions for reading text files
- Erik and Emily learn about databases
- Simon helps Emily and Erik change the application to use a database

"Let's make our project a bit more serious," Simon said when the friends met the next time.

"Yesterday, you said something about a database," Erik said. "Is that what you mean?"

"Yes, that too," Simon answered. "But first, I suggest we make changes in our folder structure. Let's organize our files. Look at our files and folders."

He took a piece of paper and started drawing and explaining.

"When we started with the Mu editor, it placed all our programs in its default folder, which is mu_code. Then we discovered that it also has all the necessary templates for web applications under the templates folder inside mu_code. If you look at it in the file manager—Finder on macOS or Explorer on Windows—you'll see that it also has more folders, such as static, images, fonts, and so on. Remember, we already created a couple of templates ourselves, order.html and print.html, and we placed them under templates. If you look into the static folder, you'll find the css folder—I think you, Emily, know that it's for style sheets—and there are a couple of files there.

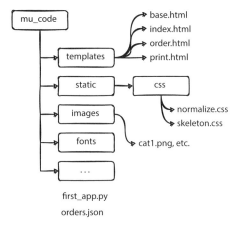

"You see, our application has several files in different folders. I suggest we create our own folder for the Coffee Shop application and copy all the files we need into that folder. That will also help us separate our web-based Coffee Shop application from our previous version. It's always a good practice to keep your different projects in separate folders."

Simon continued, "Let's create a folder for all our projects—including future projects. Usually, I name it Projects, similar to the Downloads, Pictures, and Documents folders that we already have. Under Projects, we'll create another folder and call it coffeeshop. We'll move all the files related to our web-based coffee shop project to it. I also suggest renaming first_app.py to just app.py. That's what people usually call their Flask applications. Let me show you what I mean." Simon added another diagram to the one he created before.

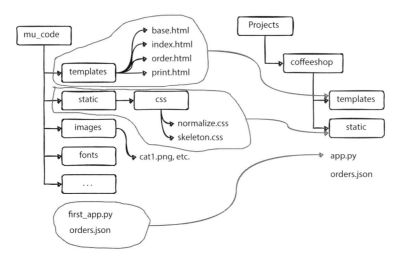

"Do you know how to do it?" Simon asked Emily and Erik.

"Yes," Emily said. They started working on creating folders and moving files. After a while, they showed Simon their `coffeeshop` project folder.

"Does this look good?" Erik asked.

```
<   >   coffeeshop                        88  :≡  |||

  Name

  📄 app.py
> 📁 fonts
> 📁 images
  📄 orders.json
∨ 📁 static
  ∨ 📁 css
        📄 normalize.css
        📄 skeleton.css
  ∨ 📁 img
        🖼 logo.png
∨ 📁 templates
      📄 base.html
      📄 index.html
      📄 order.html
      📄 print.html
```

> ### *Your Turn!* **Create your application folder**
> Create a folder for your projects (you can use the name `Projects` or some other name). Create another folder for your application. Name it according to your application—it could be `icecream` or `pizzaplace`. Move the files related to the web application from `mu_code` to this new folder.

"Let me see," Simon said, looking at their folder. "You moved your `static` directory, with all its content, and your `templates` directory, good. You even moved `fonts` and `images`—we don't use them now, but that's okay."

"I have a question," Erik said. "Why do you sometimes say 'directories' and sometimes 'folders'? I guess they mean the same, right?"

"Sorry, I don't follow strict terminology," Simon said. "You're right, those two words mean the same thing: something that holds files. They are used to organize files that belong to a certain project, like `coffeeshop`; or they're used for files of a certain type, like `templates`. Historically, in Unix and Linux systems, they are called directories. MacOS is based on Unix, and, in my robotics club, we use Linux, so I'm used to calling them directories. In Windows, they're called folders—it's exactly the same thing. Just get used to the different terms, it's not a big deal."

"Also, yesterday you said that we can keep our menus in text files, like we did in our previous version," Erik said. "For the shop manager who doesn't know HTML, remember?"

"Thanks for reminding me, Erik," Simon said. "I'm going to show you how to work with a database today. But it's a serious subject. Let's warm up with these menu files first. Can you copy them to your new directory from `mu_code`?"

"Yes, just a second," Erik said. He copied the files `drinks.txt`, `flavors.txt`, and `toppings.txt` to the `coffeeshop` project folder.

> ### *Your Turn!* **Move the menu files**
> Move the menu files to the new folder you just created.

"Now take a look at our old program and see how we worked with these files," Simon said. "Open the `menu_files.py` file and refresh your memory. Try to explain it to Emily—that's the best way to understand something better."

"Yes, I'd love to learn what you did with this program before," Emily said.

Erik looked at the code and started explaining, "We created a function called `read_menu()` that would read a text file with drinks, flavors, or toppings, and create a list of menu choices. We passed that list to the `menu()` function. The `menu()` function printed the list and asked the customer to choose the drink, then the flavor, then the topping. After all that, we printed the order."

Listing 12.1   `menu_files.py`: Read menu items from files

```
def read_menu(filename):
    f = open(filename)
    temp = f.readlines()
    result = []
    for item in temp:
        new_item = item.strip()
        result.append(new_item)

    return result

drinks = read_menu("drinks.txt")
flavors = read_menu("flavors.txt")
toppings = read_menu("toppings.txt")

drink = menu(drinks)
flavor = menu(flavors, "Erik's flavors", "Choose your flavor: ")
topping = menu(toppings, "Erik's toppings", "Choose your topping: ")

print("Here is your order: ")
print("Main product: ", drink)
print("Flavor: ", flavor)
print("Topping: ", topping)
print("Thanks for your order!")
```

"I see," Emily said. "What is a *list*? Is it like an *array* in JavaScript?"

"Yes, exactly," Simon confirmed. "It's the same thing: a collection of items placed in order. It's called different names in different programming languages, but it's the same thing. The most important thing is that you can pick items by their position in the list: like item number three or item number five. These numbers are called the *indices* of the list."

"Can we use this function again?" Erik asked.

"Of course!" Simon said. "This is what functions are created for—to reuse! Let's copy this `read_menu()` function to our new `app.py` file. Place it right after the `load_orders()` function. Also, copy the three function calls that go right after the function. We need to create these lists here too."

Erik copied the `read_menu()` function and the three lines after it from `menu_files.py` to `app.py` in the `coffeeshop` directory.

"Now we have the lists of menu choices from these three files: `drinks.txt`, `flavors.txt`, and `toppings.txt`. We have to display the choices on our order page. The good thing is that our `order.html` file is not a plain HTML file, but a *template*. We can use *variables* in the template and pass the *values* that we want to display. Remember, we did this in the `print.html` template when we passed the `new_order` dictionary. Let me remind you. Here is the Python code for that in `app.py`:

```
return render_template(
    "print.html", new_order=new_order
)
```

"And here is the part of the `order.html` template that uses the `new_order` dictionary," Simon continued.

```
. . .
<h2>Here is your order:</h2>

<p>Drink: <strong>{{ new_order["drink"] }}</strong></p>
<p>Flavor: <strong>{{ new_order["flavor"] }}</strong></p>
<p>Topping: <strong>{{ new_order["topping"] }}</strong></p>
. . .
```

"Now we should use the `order.html` template and pass the lists with choices to it. In the template, we'll use them to build the menus. Find the `render_template()` function call that uses the `order.html` template and pass these three lists the same way you passed the `new_order` dictionary a couple of lines above."

Erik found that line (it was the last line of the program) and changed it to this:

```
return render_template("order.html", drinks=drinks, flavors=flavors, toppings
    =toppings)
```

"Good," Simon said. "Now, after we have passed the lists to the template, we have to change the template. Emily, you'll be surprised. It won't look like plain HTML. We'll use *loops* in the template."

"Like in Python?" Erik said.

"Yes, they look much the same, and they work similarly," Simon said. "Instead of printing the options in our `select` menu as strings, we'll take them from the list. Our loops will look like `for d in drinks`—much like what you did in your `menu()` function. I think that's because the template language was created by the same person who created Flask—Armin Ronacher. So it's very close to Python, as you can imagine. The template language, by the way, is called *Jinja*—yes, like ninja."

"Let me help you with the `order.html` template," Simon continued. "I collected some examples, so I'll use them here."

"So you don't know *everything* yourself?" Erik winked at his brother.

"Of course not," Simon answered seriously. "I'm learning, myself. When I need something, I search the internet for examples and documentation, and I use them. Luckily, the Flask and Jinja documentation is well written and very helpful. Also, there are plenty of examples and tutorials that people have shared:"

Simon changed the `templates/order.html` file to the following:

Listing 12.2   `order.html`: Use menu lists to display menu items in the template

```
. . .
<form action="/order" method="post">
    <input type="text" name="name" placeholder="ENTER NAME">
    <select name="drink">
      <option value="">- Choose drink -</option>   ◁——— Instruction option
```

```
    {% for d in drinks -%}
    <option value="{{ d }}">{{ d | capitalize }}</option>
    {% endfor %}
  </select>
  <select name="flavor">
    <option value="">- Choose flavor -</option>
    {% for f in flavors -%}
    <option value="{{ f }}">{{ f | capitalize }}</option>
    {% endfor %}
  </select>
  <select name="topping">
    <option value="">- Choose topping -</option>
    {% for t in toppings -%}
    <option value="{{ t }}">{{ t | capitalize }}</option>
    {% endfor %}
  </select>
  <input type="submit" value="Submit">
</form>
. . .
```

> A for loop includes options from the list in the menu.

> ### *Your Turn!*   Change `order.html`
> Change your `templates/order.html` template the same way. Be careful when copying the text—note that we use *double* curly braces in templates. Don't forget all the dashes and percent signs.

They tested the page, and it worked the same way as before. Simon suggested, "Emily, try adding something to one of the menu text files, and let's see if the page is updated."

Emily opened the `toppings.txt` file and added `vanilla powder` at the end of the file. She saved the file and restarted the application. Indeed, they saw the new topping item in the menu.

> ### *Your Turn!*   Test your page
> Test your page with the new template. Does it look the same as before? Add a new item to one of the files with a text editor. Test the menus again and check if the new item is displayed.

"Simon, I see that you added that `capitalize` word in the template," she said, "and now it shows `Vanilla powder` with a capital 'V'. Pretty cool!"

"Yes," Simon said, "there are a lot of interesting things you can do with templates. That's just one of them. We can use something else later, if you want. But now we're going to learn about databases!

"Do you know why we need databases?" Simon asked. "We used a JSON file to store our orders, and it worked pretty well, right? But imagine that we want to find all orders with vanilla flavor in our list of orders, for example. Or all orders from all customers whose name is Alex. Or find out if we used more peppermint flavor this month or in the previous one. We could write such functions ourselves, right? But it turns out that questions like these are so common that people long ago started creating special programs that not only store data like orders and customers, but that can also answer such questions. These questions are usually called *queries* in the database world. Many years ago, some smart people created a language called *Structured Query Language*, or *SQL* for short. People usually pronounce it *sequel*.

"We're not going to learn SQL today," Simon continued, "but the reason I'm telling you this is that we're going to use a database called SQLite—call it *sequelight* if you want."

"Are we going to use the database instead of a JSON file to load and store orders?" Erik asked.

"Yes," Simon answered, "but we don't have to load orders anymore. Remember, we had to load orders into a list to be able to add new orders to that list and to save that list in a JSON file when we were done? Now the database will keep all our orders in its own file. The database knows how to add a new record to the list of orders, so we don't have to worry about that."

"I like it," Erik said. "What should we do now?"

Simon started drawing a diagram. "We'll use a database file called `orders.db`. We don't need the `load_orders()` function anymore." He crossed it out with a red marker.

"We don't need the list of orders—the database will keep that for us. We'll also rewrite our `save_orders()` function. We don't have to save *all* the orders in the file each time we have a new order. We'll just save the new order in the database—all previous orders will already be there. I suggest renaming the function to `save_order()`.

"Look at the diagram and see the difference between our old way of using a JSON file and the new way with a database.

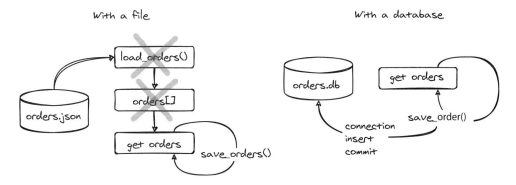

"Each time we want to save a new order, we create a *connection* to the database. Then we issue a special command to *insert* our new order into the database. After that, we call a special `commit()` function to make sure our order is saved in the database."

"It's like what we did with the file," Erik said.

"Yes, pretty similar," Simon agreed. "The difference is that now we talk to the database, not to the file. We're working on a very simple program, but what if we had more than one barista who accepts orders in our coffee shop? If several people start writing to the same file at the same time, it creates a lot of problems. When we work with a database, the database takes care of that. Even better, if you learn how to work with SQLite using the SQL language, you can also use that language with many other databases. They will understand SQL just fine."

"Enough theory, let's write some code," Simon said. "First of all, we should create a *table* in our database. In our case, the table is pretty simple—it contains the customer's name and our usual options: drink, flavor, and topping."

He started editing the `app.py` file and explaining. "I added the `import sqlite3` line at the beginning. Then I removed the `orders = load_orders()` function call and the whole `load_orders()` function. Just before the `app = Flask()` line, I added three lines that make a connection to the database and create the table called `orders`."

```
. . .
import sqlite3    ⊲──── Imports the sqlite3 package
. . .
con = sqlite3.connect("orders.db")    ⊲──── Connects to the database
cur = con.cursor()
cur.execute(
    "CREATE TABLE IF NOT EXISTS orders(name, drink, flavor, topping);")  ⊲─┐
                                                                          │
app = Flask(name)                              Creates the orders table   │
. . .
```

> ### Your Turn!   Add commands to connect to a database and create a table
> Change your `app.py` file and add the three lines like Simon did. Don't forget to add `import sqlite3` at the very beginning of your `app.py` file.

"What is `cur`?" Emily asked.

"It's called a *cursor* in the database world. Like your mouse cursor, it can point to a specific place in a database. We're not going to go into the details—in this case, I'm following the examples from the official Python documentation. The documentation says we need this cursor to execute SQL commands in the database.

"Look at the next line with `cur.execute()`. This is our first SQL instruction. It creates a table called `orders` with *columns* named `name`, `drink`, `flavor`, and `topping`. In databases, tables are just normal tables with rows and columns. Each new order is a new row in the table. In each row, we have four columns with names that I mentioned already. Easy, huh?" He drew a simple table.

"Now let's rewrite the `save_orders()` function. First, we'll rename it to `save_order()` because we're going to save just one order at a time. Then, we'll repeat the two lines I wrote earlier to create a connection and create a cursor. After that, we can execute the SQL command. In this case, we'll use the `INSERT` command and pass the values from the `order[]` dictionary. Finally, we'll call the `commit()` function to save the new order in the database."

Listing 12.3   `app.py`: Add orders to the table

```
. . .
from flask import Flask, render_template, request

def save_order(order):
    con = sqlite3.connect("orders.db")
    cur = con.cursor()
    cur.execute(
    "INSERT INTO orders(name,drink,flavor,topping) VALUES(?,?,?,?);",
    (order["name"], order["drink"], order["flavor"], order["topping"]),
    )
    con.commit()
    return
. . .
```

Your Turn!   Create a `save_order()` function
Copy the `save_order()` function to your program. Pay attention to quotes, square brackets, commas, and parentheses.

"I know, it looks complicated, but if you just read it, it's pretty easy to understand. You tell the database to `INSERT` some `VALUES` into the `orders` database. Then you list those values in parentheses. You're already familiar with dictionaries, and you know how to pull a *value* for a certain *key*."

"Why did you write some words in all caps?" Erik asked.

"It's a convention in SQL. People use all caps for SQL commands and keywords, like `INSERT` and `INTO`. For variables, like the table name `orders`, people use lowercase letters. I tried using lowercase for commands too and it worked. So the capitals are just a readability convention to separate SQL words from variables."

"Let's try it!" Emily said.

"Wait!" Simon said. "I almost forgot—we should remove the `load_orders()` call from the `order()` function. And we should rename the save function too."

He edited the `order()` function so it looked like this:

```python
@app.route("/order", methods=("GET", "POST"))
def order():
    if request.method == "POST":
        new_order = {"name": request.form["name"],
                     "drink": request.form["drink"],
                     "flavor": request.form["flavor"],
                     "topping": request.form["topping"]
                     }
        save_order(new_order)
        return render_template(
            "print.html", new_order=new_order
        )

    return render_template("order.html", drinks=drinks,
                           flavors=flavors, toppings=toppings)
```

Your Turn!   **Edit your `order()` function**
Edit your `order()` function the same way Simon did. Don't forget to change `save _orders()` (plural) to `save_order()` (singular).

He saved the file and said, "Ready now. Emily, run it! But let me fill the order, okay?"
    Emily clicked Run and reloaded the order page. Simon entered the menu choices.

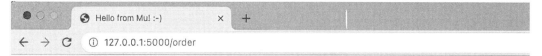

Hello Simon!

Here is your order:

Drink: **coffee**

Flavor: **caramel**

Topping: **chocolate**

NEW ORDER

> ### *Your Turn!*   Test it
> Test your program. Now it uses a database instead of a JSON file, but the interface should look the same.

"It works!" Simon said, with a sigh of relief. He wasn't sure himself that he'd done everything right, and he didn't want to show that.

"Can we check if the order was saved in the database, like we did with the JSON file?" Erik asked.

"Good question!" Simon said. "No, the database file is not a text file that we can read. But we can do better. We can create a new function that will show us all the orders on the web page."

"That would be great!" Erik said. "For example, if a shop manager wants to see how many portions of caramel we have used today."

"And we could see what a particular customer likes to order," Emily added.

"Great ideas," Simon said. "Are you ready to work a little more? We'll need three things. First, remember that to open the order page, we add /order to the site address. In Flask, that's called a *route*. We should create a function for a new route that we can use to list the orders."

"Let's call this route /list. The function for this route will also be called list(). It's very similar to the order() function. At the end of this list() function, we'll also call the render_template() function to display the list of orders."

"Second," he continued, "we'll create a function that will talk to the database and return the list of orders to the list() function. Let's call it get_orders()."

"And third, we should create a template to display the orders. Emily, did you learn how to create tables in HTML?"

"Tables? Yes, I can do that," Emily said. "We should use the <table> tag to create a table, then the <tr> tag for each row, and the <td> tag for each cell in the row."

"Great!" Simon said. "Then you'll create the template for our list() function. Erik, you write the functions, okay?"

"Sure," Erik said. "Where should I start?"

"Right after the save_order() function. Create a function called get_orders(). Start with the same first line as in the save_order() function. Add one more line after it: con.row_factory = sqlite3.Row. It's a special instruction that allows us to use column names when working with the result. Don't worry about it now—you'll see it later. Then, create a cursor with the same line as before: cur = con.cursor(). Let me see your code."

Erik showed what he had written:

```
def get_orders():
    con = sqlite3.connect("orders.db")
    con.row_factory = sqlite3.Row
    cur = con.cursor()
```

"Good," Simon said. "Now the important part: we have to get all the orders from the table called `orders`. We'll use one of the most common SQL instructions, which tells the database to give us all rows and all columns from a table. It looks like this: `SELECT * FROM orders;`. The asterisk `*` means 'everything.'

"We should use this instruction with the same `cur.execute()` function that we used in `save_order()`. After we execute the instruction, the results should be *fetched* from the database. You'll have to store the results in the list called `rows` using the `cur.fetchall()` function. Then, you'll return the list of rows from this function.

"Don't worry, here is the documentation page I'm getting it from. Use it as an example." Simon showed the tab he had open in the browser: https://docs.python.org/3.8/library/sqlite3.html.

Erik started typing. After several minutes, he showed his code to Simon:

Listing 12.5   `app.py`: The `get_orders()` function

```
def get_orders():
    con = sqlite3.connect("orders.db")
    con.row_factory = sqlite3.Row
    cur = con.cursor()
    cur.execute("SELECT * FROM orders;")
    rows = cur.fetchall()

    return rows
```

> ***Your Turn!***   **Create a `get_orders()` function**
> Create a `get_orders()` function like Erik just did.

"Looks good to me," Simon said. "We'll see when we test it.

"Now we have to add another function that handles the `/list` route. We should add it after the `order()` function that handles `/order`. Let me help you." He started writing the function at the end of the file.

"First, I specify the route we're going to handle using `@app.route()`. Then, I define the function the usual way. The function itself is pretty simple: I just call `get_orders()` and pass the results to `render_template()`. As you'll remember, this function displays the data in the browser using the template we pass to it."

Listing 12.6   `app.py`: Create the `list()` function

```
@app.route("/list", methods=["GET"])
def list():
    orders = get_orders()

    return render_template("list.html", orders=orders)
```

> ### *Your Turn!* **Create a `list()` function**
> Create a `list()` function like Erik just did.

"Why didn't we get all the orders from the database right in this function?" Erik asked. "Why did you ask me to write a separate function?"

"Good question," Simon said. "I'm trying to separate the functions that work with the *user* from the functions that work with the *data*. Sometimes people call this the *frontend* and *backend*. If we want to change how we work with data, we have to change the `get_orders()` function. For example, suppose we wanted to be able to get only the orders with caramel flavor. We would pass that request to the function, and it would return the list of orders the same way as before. Our `list()` function will display whatever it gets from `get_orders()`. It doesn't care if it's the full list of orders, or just some of the orders—it just displays them. On the other hand, the `get_orders()` function doesn't care about how the orders will be displayed. It just returns the list of orders.

"This idea is usually called the *separation of concerns* in computer science. I'll give you a Wikipedia article about that to read later.

NOTE The Wikipedia article about the separation of concerns is here: https://en.wikipedia.org/wiki/Separation_of_concerns.

"The only thing that's left is the list template," Simon said. "Emily, let's start a new file in the editor. Remove the sample web application that Mu created for us. Save your new file under `templates` with the name `list.html`. Don't forget to change the file type from 'Python (*.py)' to 'Other (*.*)'.

"Start with the same template lines that we used in the `print.html` template. The first two lines and the last line should be the same."

Emily copied these three lines:

```
{% extends "base.html" %}
{% block content %}

{% endblock %}
```

"Now create a table with one empty row and empty cells. We'll have four cells in each row and four column headers. That will be the first row. Do you know how to create column headers?" Simon asked Emily.

"Yes, with the `<th>` tag," she answered. She started working on an HTML table in the `templates/list.html` file.

"You can add the headers now," Simon said. "There will be `Name`, `Drink`, `Flavor`, and `Topping`.

Listing 12.7   The `templates/list.html` template with headers

```
{% extends "base.html" %}
{% block content %}

<table>
    <tr>
        <th>Name</th>
        <th>Drink</th>
        <th>Flavor</th>
        <th>Topping</th>
    </tr>
    <tr>
        <td></td>
        <td></td>
        <td></td>
        <td></td>
    </tr>
</table>
{% endblock %}
```

"Great," Simon said. "Now let me add the loop. We'll use the same `for` loop here that we used to display the menus. Remember, we pass the list called `orders` to this template. The loop will go over that list, like this: `for o in orders`. In each cell, between `<td>` and `</td>`, we'll insert the value for each of the keys: `name`, `drink`, `flavor`, and `topping`." Simon changed the template:

Listing 12.8   The `templates/list.html` template with the `for` loop

```
{% extends "base.html" %}
{% block content %}

<table>
    <tr>
        <th>Name</th>
        <th>Drink</th>
        <th>Flavor</th>
        <th>Topping</th>
    </tr>
    {% for o in orders -%}
    <tr>
        <td>{{ o['name'] }}</td>
        <td>{{ o['drink'] }}</td>
        <td>{{ o['flavor'] }}</td>
        <td>{{ o['topping'] }}</td>
    </tr>
    {% endfor %}
</table>
{% endblock %}
```

> **Your Turn!   Create a list template**
>
> Create a `templates/list.html` file like Emily just did. Pay attention to quotes, square brackets, and double curly braces.

"It's time to try the list function!" Simon said, after he saved the file. "Start the application and enter two or three orders."

Erik started the application, opened the tab with `127.0.0.1:5000/order`, and entered three orders: for Simon, for Emily, and for himself.

"Now, change that `/order` route in the address to `/list`," Simon said.

Erik did, and they saw the result.

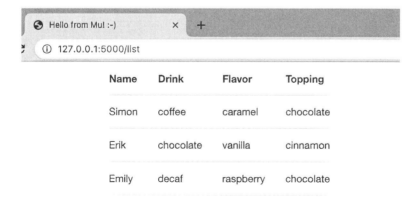

"Looks great," Emily said. "Very useful for a shop manager!"

"Yes, I like it too," Erik said. "I think we should add numbers to the rows to see how many people we have served."

"Great idea!" Simon said. "And you can add dates and times to see how many customers you served each day. It's all possible—we just have to change our database to keep this information. But we'll do that later. For tomorrow, I have another idea. Emily, do you know CSS by any chance?"

"We learned a little bit in our class," Emily answered.

"What is CSS?" Erik asked.

"It's a way to change how your HTML page looks in the browser," Emily explained. "I think it stands for *Cascading Style Sheets*."

"Exactly right," Simon said. "Tomorrow, let's work on making our site look even better with CSS. But before you go, let's recap what we did today."

Emily started, "We created a new project directory and moved all our content into it. We renamed the main application file to `app.py`."

"We used the text files for menu items the same way we did in the previous version," Erik added. "Now the shop manager can simply edit those files instead of changing the program."

"And then we started using the database," Emily said. "It's not easy."

"Yes, I agree," Simon said. "But it's worth it. With the database, our program is more professional. Now it's time to make it more beautiful. We'll work on that tomorrow."

New things you have learned today

- *Folders and directories*—In different operating systems, people use different terms for the same thing. Folders and directories are both collections of files that belong to a certain project or files of a certain type.

- *Jinja templates*—Jinja templates are used by Flask to create HTML pages. You can pass variables, lists, and dictionaries into templates and use them as you would in Python. You can use `for` loops in templates, similar to in Python.

- *Database*—A database is a program that can store data and perform various operations on the data. Databases can search records using specific criteria or summarize data (like the number of vanilla flavor orders for this month).

- *SQL*—SQL stands for Structured Query Language, and it's used to work with databases.

- *Frontend and backend*—The frontend part of an application works with users: it displays pages and gets input from the keyboard and menus. The backend part works with data: it stores and retrieves data from files and databases. The frontend and backend parts are used to separate the concerns when working on big applications.

Code for this chapter

You can find the code for this chapter here: https://github.com/pavelanni/pythonicadventure-code/tree/main/ch12.

Styles: Making it pretty

## 13

In this chapter

- Erik and Emily experiment with styles, colors, and fonts
- Erik and Emily create a new home page for the shop
- Erik and Emily add pictures to their pages

"Let's make it pretty!" Simon said when the friends met the next time.

"You mean—using styles for our HTML files?" Emily asked. "We used styles in our HTML class. You can change colors, font sizes, and backgrounds. It's pretty neat!"

Simon said, "Yes, let's talk about styles. Emily, can you explain a little bit?"

"It's called CSS. And it stands for . . . ," she paused for a moment, remembering. "It stands for *Cascading Style Sheets*, right?" and she looked at Simon. "But honestly, I don't remember why."

"You're right!" Simon said. "Cascading Style Sheets it is! They are called *style sheets* because they are just plain text files describing styles. Styles specify the ways your HTML elements look on the page. For example, you can say that your `<h2>` headers should have a size of 36 pixels and should be red. Or they should use a specific font."

He continued, "One of the ideas in web design is separating content from styles. Of course, we could set the style in the HTML file. But that is not very convenient. If you want to change the font size or color, you'd have to go through *all* your HTML files and change *all* the <h2> headers. Instead of that, we define styles in a separate file, where we say all <h2> headers should use this color and size. Then, if we want to change it, we only need to change it in one place. Very convenient, huh?"

"I see," Erik said. "It's like functions in Python. You write it once, and then you use it in other places."

"Yes, right!" Simon said. "I like your analogy. So, we figured out why they are called style sheets, but why *cascading*? For your web site or application, you can have several style sheets and combine them, one after another. Often, people use a style sheet created by somebody else and add or change only the elements that they want to look different. This is another similarity to functions."

He continued, "In our project, we'll use the style sheets included in the Mu editor, and we'll change them a little to make them more appropriate for our coffee shop project. Take a look at your order page and think about what we should change."

Erik looked at the screen and said, "We need a title. Like in our terminal application: Welcome to Erik's Coffee Shop!"

"Wait!" Emily said. "It's not just your coffee shop anymore. I think it should be called Erik and Emily's Coffee Shop. Or, E&E Coffee Shop for short. Agree?"

"I think it's a team project now, and E&E is a great name," Simon said.

"Yes, let's make it E&E Coffee Shop," Erik agreed.

"Let me add it," Emily said. She opened the order.html file from the templates folder. She added a title so the beginning of the file now looked like this:

```
{% extends "base.html" %}
{% block content %}

<h1>Welcome to E&E Coffee Shop</h1>

<form action="/order" method="post">
    <input type="text" name="name" placeholder="ENTER NAME">

. . .
```

Emily saved the file, switched to the app.py tab in the Mu editor, and clicked Run. She opened the browser tab and entered the URL again: http://127.0.0.1:5000/order.

"Looks good!" Erik said.

"Simon, you said that we could change the font in the title," Emily said. "This one looks a bit . . . boring. I think we need something more fancy."

"I agree," Simon said. "Luckily, there are a lot of web fonts that we can use for free. Some fonts cost money, but, for this project, free fonts are just fine. For example, Google Fonts is a good resource."

He opened a new tab in the browser and typed the address: `fonts.google.com`. "As you can see, there are more than 1,400 fonts to choose from. You can find fonts for different languages too. See this field that says 'Type something'? Enter your page title, and you'll see how it looks in different fonts."

"What about 'Categories'? What does that mean?" Emily asked.

"If you click that menu, you'll see Serif, Sans Serif, Display, Handwriting, and Monospace. Monospace is used for program code, usually. You can use Handwriting if you want to print a greeting card for a friend. Display means it's used only for computer displays and not for printing. Serif and Sans Serif sound strange, but they actually represent two classes of fonts you're very familiar with. Serif means that the font has small strokes at the ends of letters. Of course, you know Times New Roman, the default font for most programs and documents. Try choosing only Serif from the Categories menu, and you'll see what I mean."

"I like this Playfair Display!" Emily said.

"Good!" Simon said, "Make a note, and we'll get back to it. I just wanted to show you what sans serif fonts look like. 'Sans' means 'without'; in this case, it means the fonts don't have those strokes I mentioned before. Most likely, you've seen Arial from this category. Look here," and he changed the Category to Sans Serif.

"Fonts like these are used in menus and other application interface details. Just look around, and you'll start noticing and recognizing these two font categories everywhere on the web and in applications. If you want to learn more about fonts, click on the Knowledge tab. It's very interesting, believe me!"

Your Turn! **Learn more about Google Fonts**

Open the `fonts.google.com` page and look around. Try to find interesting fonts and search the different categories. Note that you can sort the output in several different ways: Trending, Most Popular, Newest, and so on. Open your favorite sites and try to figure out where they use serif, sans serif, and monospace fonts.

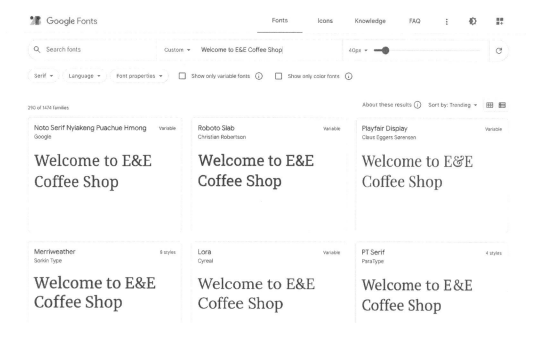

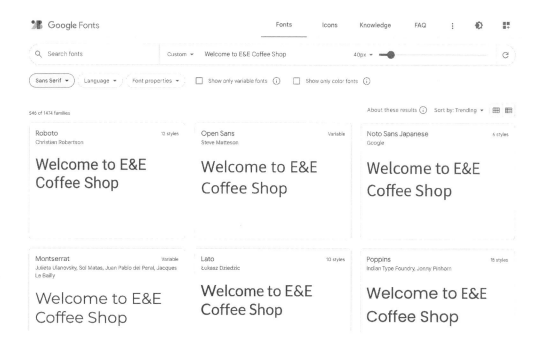

"These fonts look nice, but I like that Playfair font. I think it will be good for our page title. Erik, what do you think?" Emily asked.

"Yes, I like it too. It's not boring," Erik said. "And I like the way they made the & sign. Yes, it's good for the title."

Simon switched back to the Serif category and clicked the Playfair Display font. The font page opened. Simon explained, "Here you can find information on how to use this font in your web page or app."

He scrolled the page until the title they used appeared just below the Styles title. "Here you can select one of the font weights. As you can see, the same font, or I should say *typeface*, can have different 'boldness.' I selected just one of them, and that will give us the information we need. Notice the small red dot in the top-right corner of the page. That means we have selected something for our collection, and we should click it to open the instructions."

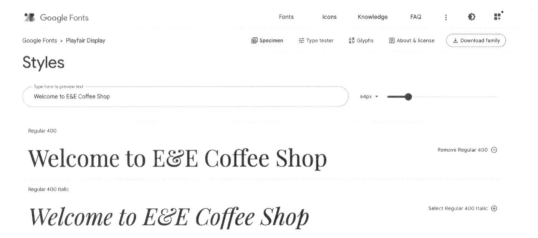

He clicked the icon with the red dot, and it showed the instructions they needed.

"Look at the block on the right, under Use On the Web. Google gives us good instructions on how to use this font. We just have to copy these lines into our files. Out of the first two pieces of code, it recommends using the first one, with `<link>`. The third piece of code, called CSS Rules to Specify Families, demonstrates how we can use this font in our CSS files. It may look complicated, but don't worry, I'll help you.

"A good thing in Flask is that we use templates," Simon continued. "Look at your `order.html` file: you'll see that it starts with `{% extends "base.html" %}`. Your `print.html` file also starts with this line. It means that we *reuse* `base.html` in our templates. We don't have to change every file in our project—we just need to change `base.html`. Yes, Erik, similar to functions again," and Simon smiled.

"Emily, would you please open the `base.html` file in the `templates` directory?"

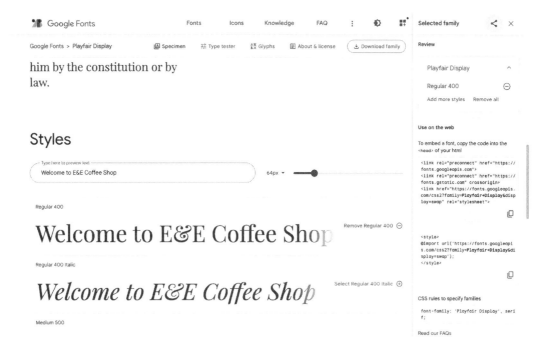

him by the constitution or by law.

Styles

When Emily opened the file, Simon said, "Look at the Google Fonts web page with the instructions. Copy the three lines that start with `<link>` from the gray box. Then paste them in `base.html`, just before the closing `</head>` tag."

Emily copied the line into the `base.html` file, and now it looked like this (I'm showing just a part of it):

Listing 13.1   `templates/base.html`: Add the font

```
. . .
  <meta name="viewport" content="width=device-width, initial-scale=1">

  <link rel="preconnect" href="https://fonts.googleapis.com">
  <link rel="preconnect" href="https://fonts.gstatic.com" crossorigin>
  <link href="https://fonts.googleapis.com/
css2?family=Playfair+Display&display=swap" rel="stylesheet">
  </head>
<body>
. . .
```

> **Your Turn!   Add the font link to `base.html`**
> Open the `templates/base.html` file in the editor and make the changes Emily just did.

"Good. That was step 1," Simon said. "Step 2 is to create our own style sheet. Click New in the editor. It will create an example web application, but we don't need that now. Remove all the text in it and click Save. You should save it in the same directory where the other CSS files are stored, under `static/css`. Name the file `coffeeshop.css`. Don't forget to change the file extension from 'Python (*.py)' to 'Other (*.*)'."

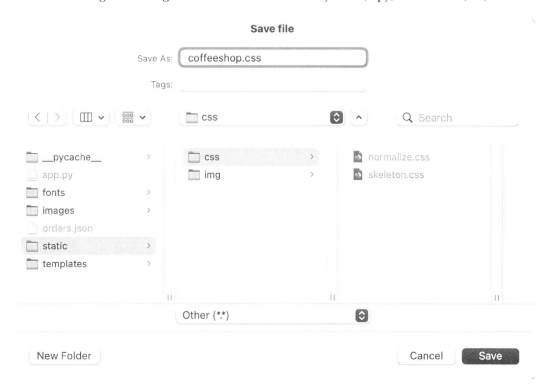

Simon checked that the `coffeeshop.css` file appeared next to the other CSS files. "Good," he said. "Now we can add the font specification to the `h1` header.

"Look at the CSS Rules to Specify Families box on the font page in the browser. Select and copy the text from there. Now type `h1 {` and paste what you copied after the opening curly brace. Then add the closing curly brace and save the file."

That was easy. Emily edited the `coffeeshop.css` file so it looked like this:

Listing 13.2   static/css/coffeeshop.css: Add font to CSS

```
h1 {font-family: 'Playfair Display', serif;}
```

Your Turn!   Create `coffeeshop.css`
Create the `static/css/coffeeshop.css` file in the editor and add the line for the `h1` style.

"Great!" Simon said. "Now we have our own CSS file. We just have to tell Flask that we want to use it. That's step 3. I guess you still have `base.html` open in the editor, Emily? Find the two lines with the word `stylesheet`. You'll recognize the names."

"Yes, I see them," Emily said. "They are called `normalize.css` and `skeleton.css`—the same names I saw when I saved our style sheet."

"Good, now copy the line with `skeleton.css` and paste it right after itself. You should have two lines that are exactly the same. Now, in the second of them, change `skeleton` to `coffeeshop`."

Emily did, and now the `base.html` file looked like this:

Listing 13.3 `templates/base.html`: Add the `coffeeshop` CSS file

```
. . .
<!-- CSS
---------------------------------------------- -->
<link rel="stylesheet" href="/static/css/normalize.css">
<link rel="stylesheet" href="/static/css/skeleton.css">
<link rel="stylesheet" href="/static/css/coffeeshop.css">
. . .
```

> ***Your Turn!*** **Add the `coffeeshop.css` style sheet to `base.html`**
> Open the `templates/base.html` file in the editor and make the changes Emily just did.

"Now you can see why these style sheets are called *cascading*. We have three style sheets. The first one, called `normalize.css`, is needed to make sure our web site will look good on all kinds of browsers on different devices."

"Even on my iPad?" Erik asked.

"Yes, it should," Simon answered. "We'll test it later."

He continued, "The next CSS file is called `skeleton.css`. It was included with the Mu editor and provides good-looking styles for all HTML elements. We don't have to create styles for single elements—they look good already. We only need to add styles to our own CSS file if we want to change something, like the font family for headers. The styles are applied one after another, in the order the CSS files are listed in the HTML file. That's why they are called cascading.

NOTE You can read more about `normalize.css` here: https://nicolasgallagher .com/about-normalize-css/. The `skeleton.css` style sheet is described here: http://getskeleton.com/.

"Enough theory, let's take a look at our website!" Simon said.

Emily and Erik checked again that they had saved all the files. Then they switched to the `app.py` tab and clicked Run. They opened the browser tab with the familiar address `http://127.0.0.1:5000/order`, and they saw the updated page.

Welcome to E&E Coffee Shop

"Wow! I love it!" Erik exclaimed.

"Now you know how to change any font on your web page," Simon said.

"But why does it say 'Hello from Mu!'?" Erik noticed. "Shouldn't it be 'Hello from E&E'?"

"Good point!" Simon said. "That's pretty easy to change. Find the phrase in the `base.html` file and change it. It should be very close to the beginning, enclosed in the `<title>` tags."

Erik quickly found the phrase and changed it. "Should I restart the Python application?" he asked Simon.

"No, you can just reload the page in your browser, and you'll see the change."

Indeed, the page now showed the new title.

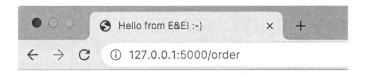

Emily said, "We can also change the background color. I think we need something that looks like coffee or cappuccino."

"Great idea!" Simon said. "First, you have to find a good color that you both like. The simplest way is to open a Google search page and type `color picker`."

Simon did just that to demonstrate it and they saw the Color Picker.

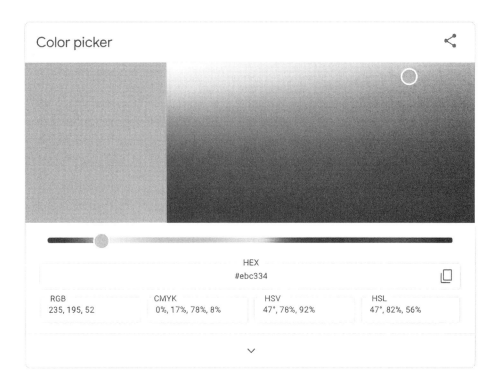

"You can use the rainbow line to choose the base color, and then use the white circle to pick the shade you like.

"There are many other sites that can help you pick good combinations of colors. It's a whole world—the same as with fonts. There is plenty to learn. For example," and he chose one of the first results from the search page: https://htmlcolorcodes .com/color-picker/. "Try it too, and you'll find a lot of useful information about colors and how to use them for web pages."

Erik and Emily spent several minutes playing with the Color Picker and finally came up with a color.

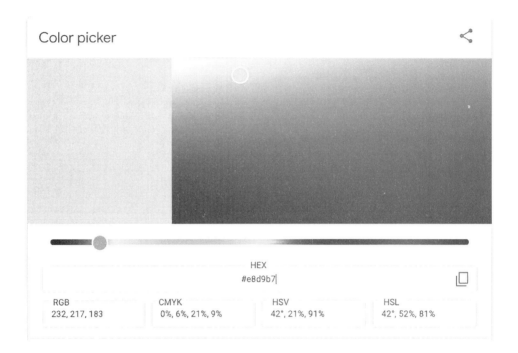

Your Turn!   Play with the Color Picker

Find the Color Picker in Google and play with it. Figure out how to change the base color and then how to change how light or dark it is. Find your favorite colors for a background.

"Good," Simon said. "Now copy these six letters and numbers under Hex, and we'll edit the `coffeeshop.css` file. Who's typing this time?"

"I am," Erik said.

"Enter this: `body {background-color:`. Then paste what you copied from the Color Picker. Make sure you included the hash sign (`#`). Then enter a semicolon and close the curly brace."

Erik added the line, so now the CSS file looked like this:

Listing 13.4   `static/css/coffeeshop.css`: Add a background color to CSS

```
h1 {font-family: 'Playfair Display', serif;}

body {background-color: #e8d9b7;}
```

Your Turn!   Change your page background

Edit your `static/css/coffeeshop.css` file and add the `body` line with the background color of your choice.

Erik reloaded the orders page, and now it looked much different.

"I like it more and more," Emily said. "Can we make these menus the same coffee color too?"

"Yes, sure," Simon answered. "But I suggest making them a bit lighter in tone, not exactly the same color. Go ahead and find something."

That was even easier. Emily and Erik ended up with a new tone for the menus.

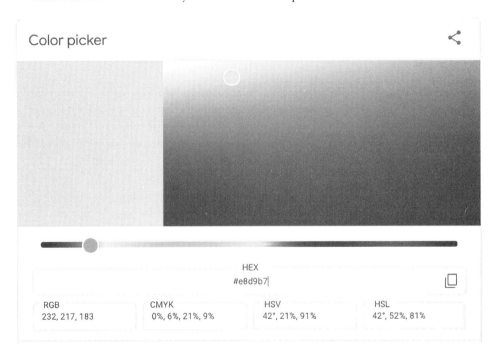

"Good. Now let me help you to add it to the style sheet," Simon said. "We should apply this color to the elements of our form. The menu element is called `select`, and the input field where you enter the customer's name is called `input[type="text"]`. Let's add them to the style sheet and use the background color you chose:

```
input[type="text"], select {background-color: #ede9df;}
```

"What are these numbers and letters? What do they mean?" Erik asked.

"They mean that you can describe any color you want with these six numbers and letters," Emily explained. "The six consist of three pairs for three colors: red, green, and blue. Each pair says how much of that color is in the color we chose. It's like with paints: you can mix red and blue to get purple. Each pair of symbols is a number, but in hex, and they can be numbers or letters from a to f. I just don't remember why it's called 'hex'."

"Hex is short for hexadecimal," Simon said. "It's a way to represent numbers, similar to our normal way, but shorter and more understandable by computers. In our usual system, called 'decimal,' we have digits from 0 to 9, for a total of 10 digits. With one digit we can describe the numbers from 0 to 9. With two digits we can describe the numbers from 0 to 99. The hexadecimal system is similar, but instead of 10 digits, we have 16 digits. They go from 0 to f: we added the letters from a to f and use them as digits. So, the digit a means 10, b means 11, and so on. The digit f means 15. With one hexadecimal digit, we can describe the numbers from 0 to 15; with two, from 0 to 255. And it's shorter: 255 requires three digits in the decimal system, but in hexadecimal it's just ff.

"Let's get back to colors," Simon continued. "As Emily said, each 6-digit hexadecimal number tells us *how much* of red, green, and blue is in a particular color. For example, your menu's color, `#ede9df`, means a mix of `ed` of red, `e9` of green, and `df` of blue. In decimal numbers, that means . . . ," Simon looked at the Color Picker page and read the numbers from there, "it means 237 of red, 233 of green, and 223 of blue. The numbers can go up to 255. If all three of them become 255, that will be plain white."

"And if all three are 0s, that means black," Emily added.

"Exactly right," Simon confirmed. "If you want to learn more about web colors, read the Wikipedia article about them." He quickly found the Web Colors page and opened it in a new tab: https://en.wikipedia.org/wiki/Web_colors.

"I want to order something from our new design," Emily said. She entered her order. Then she clicked Submit and saw the new page.

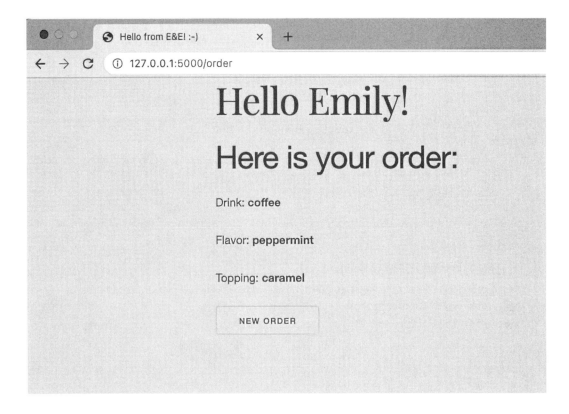

"Why didn't it print the second line in our font?" she was not very pleased.

"Maybe because we just set the font for `h1`?" Erik suggested.

"You're right, Erik," Simon said. "It's pretty easy to fix. Open the `skeleton.css` file and look at how the styles are defined there. We can learn a lot by looking at how it's done in other people's style sheets. Go ahead and find the section called `Typography`. You'll see how to style other header levels."

Erik opened `skeleton.css` and scrolled to `Typography`. He saw this:

Listing 13.6   `static/css/skeleton.css`: The `Typography` section

```
/* Typography
-------------------------------------------------- */
h1, h2, h3, h4, h5, h6 {
  margin-top: 0;
  margin-bottom: 2rem;
  font-weight: 300; }
h1 { font-size: 4.0rem; line-height: 1.2;  letter-spacing: -.1rem;}
h2 { font-size: 3.6rem; line-height: 1.25; letter-spacing: -.1rem; }
h3 { font-size: 3.0rem; line-height: 1.3;  letter-spacing: -.1rem; }
h4 { font-size: 2.4rem; line-height: 1.35; letter-spacing: -.08rem; }
h5 { font-size: 1.8rem; line-height: 1.5;  letter-spacing: -.05rem; }
h6 { font-size: 1.5rem; line-height: 1.6;  letter-spacing: 0; }
```

Simon said, "I'm not going into all the details here, but you can see that you can list different header levels— h1, h2, h3, and so on—separated by commas, and apply the style to all of them. Also, for each of the header levels, you can set its own font size and other parameters. You can copy this part into your `coffeeshop.css` file and try to change various parameters. But for now, the important part is that we add `h2`, `h3`, and so on to our `h1` style."

"Got it," Erik said. He quickly changed the first line of `coffeeshop.css`:

Listing 13.7   `static/css/coffeeshop.css`: Changing the font for all headers

```
h1, h2, h3, h4, h5, h6 {font-family: 'Playfair Display', serif;}
```

He clicked the Reload button, and the browser displayed a confirmation message.

Confirm Form Resubmission

The page that you're looking for used information that you entered. Returning to that page might cause any action you took to be repeated. Do you want to continue?

Cancel   Continue

"Click Continue," Simon said. "It will just submit Emily's order again. That's fine while we're testing, but in a real application, it would create another record in our database, and a new order, so you should be careful when this application is running in a real coffee shop."

Now the application showed the right font.

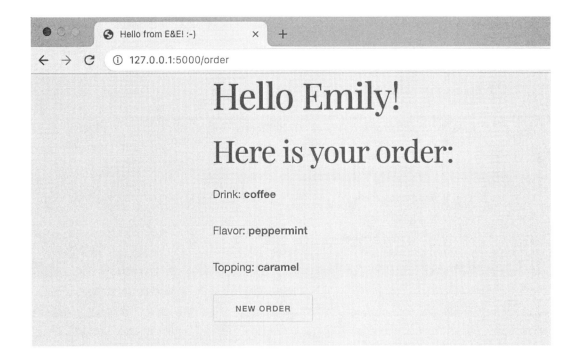

Your Turn!   Change the font for other headers

Edit your `static/css/coffeeshop.css` file to change the font for all headers from `h1` to `h6`.

"We can also add a picture," Emily said. "We did it in class. We just have to find a nice picture and download it."

"Yes, good idea," Simon said. "Make sure though that you don't download just *any* picture. There are a lot of cool pictures on the internet, but most of them have owners, like photographers or artists, who don't like it when someone takes their pictures and posts them on their own website without even mentioning the owner. There are a lot of rules around this, and different owners will have different requests. For us, it will be safe to search for free pictures, to make sure we don't violate somebody's rights. Search for something like `coffee images free download`, and let's see what it gives us."

Emily and Erik searched for several minutes, clicking on different pictures and arguing about them. Finally, Erik said, "This one is good. It has different kinds of coffee drinks, in nice cups, with toppings." And he showed Simon the page: https://www.freepik.com/free-vector/colorful-coffee-cup-set-flat-style_1544839.htm.

"Well, let's take a look," Simon said. "Look at this block on the page."

⊘ Free license   More info

✎ Attribution is required   How to attribute?

▯ File type: AI, EPS, JPG   How to edit?

He clicked "More info" and checked the license terms.

License summary

Our license allows you to use the content

✓ For commercial and **personal projects**

✓ On digital or **printed media**

✓ For an **unlimited number of times** and without any time limits

✓ From **anywhere in the world**

✓ To make **modifications** and create derivative works

"Looks good to me. We're allowed to use it, but we have to use attribution—see this `Attribution is required` phrase? Let's see what we should do." He clicked the How to Attribute? link.

How to attribute?

Creating content takes a lot of time and effort, which is why we ask you to provide a link to attribute the source. Where will you be using the image?

Web   Printed items   Video   Apps and games

For example: websites, social media, blogs, ebooks, newsletters, etc.

Copy this link and paste it in a visible place, close to where you're using the image. If that's not possible, place it at the footer of your website, blog or newsletter, or in the credits section.

Image by Freepik   Copy ▯

"We have to copy the text and add it on our page next to the picture. No problem," he said. He clicked the blue Copy button.

"Now we have to add it to our order page," he said. He opened the `order.html` file, and pasted the text at the bottom of the page, just before the `{% endblock %}` line. "We'll move it later, when we place our picture," he explained.

"Now download the picture," he said to Erik.

Erik clicked the green Download button and then the Free Download drop-down menu. He then selected JPG.

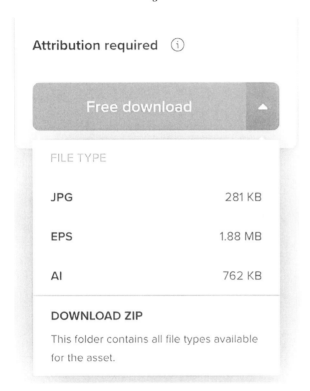

The image's filename, `1544839_222805-P1KRC2-559.jpg`, appeared at the bottom of his browser.

> **NOTE** In your case, the filename will likely be different. Please use *your* filename in the following code changes.

Simon said, "Now copy this downloaded image file from the Downloads folder to your project folder. You'll have to copy it under `coffeeshop/static/img/`. Can you find it?"

"I think so," Erik said. He opened the file manager program (Finder on his MacBook). After several mouse moves and clicks, he found the right location. His project directory now contained the image file.

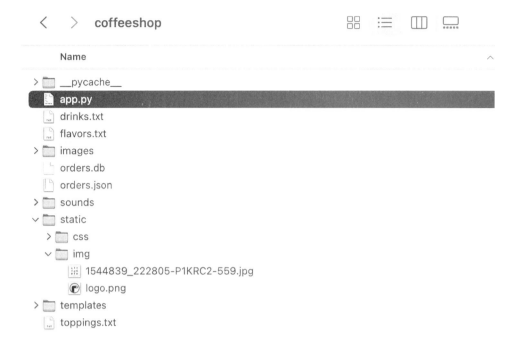

"Great," Simon said. "Now we have to place it on the page. Open the `order.html` file again. Let me help you," Simon said. He added a line just before the one with the attribution he copied earlier.

The bottom of the `order.html` file now looked like this:

```
. . .
<img src="/static/img/1544839_222805-P1KRC2-559.jpg"
 alt="Coffee drinks" width="100%">
Image by <a href="https://www.freepik.com/free-vector/
colorful-coffee-cup-set-flat-style_1544839.htm">Freepik</a>

{% endblock %}
```

He saved the file and said to Emily and Erik, "Now reload the page, and we'll see if it worked."

Emily clicked Reload, and they saw the updated page.

Your Turn!   Add a picture to your page

Find a picture you like and add it to your order page. Don't forget to check the license and follow the instructions for attribution.

"Great job!" Simon said. "It looks like a real online shop now. What's important is that it not only looks great, but it works too!"

Emily and Erik were happy to see the result of their hard work. It wasn't easy to gather all the small pieces together, but the result was overwhelming—it was a real web application that they wrote themselves.

"How about a recap?" Simon asked.

"I liked working with fonts and colors. It was easier than working with the database," Emily said. "And thanks for explaining about hexadecimal numbers—I didn't know all the details."

"I liked the Google Fonts page," Erik said. "There are so many beautiful fonts! Can I use them in my documents too? I was going to create a poster."

"Sure!" Simon answered. "You can install them on your computer and use them in Word. In Google Docs, you don't even have to install them. Just find More Fonts in the Fonts menu and use them."

"Also, we learned about picture licensing and attribution," Emily added. "Simon, you're right, it's a whole world out there."

"Good recap, great job," Simon said. "Now I have another idea. You know what AI, or *Artificial Intelligence*, is, right?"

"Yes, all those silly chatbots and programs that create funny pictures," Erik answered. "We tried some of them with friends."

"Yes, but I'm talking about AI that can help us developers," Simon said. "Some tools can help us write functions, improve our code, and explain error messages."

"Yes, I saw some demos," Emily said. "They wrote whole working programs. It looked like magic. Simon, does that mean AI can write an application like the one we just wrote?"

"Probably," Simon said. "But, it still can't do it without human help. First, you have to come up with an application idea, like Erik did several weeks ago. Second, you have to explain to the AI what you want from it. You have to be very specific, or the AI will do something that you don't expect. Third, you'll have to review the code and make sure it works as you want it to work. And, of course, no AI can choose the website colors, fonts, and pictures that *you* like, the way you just did with Erik. That's a matter of taste, and no AI can do it, as far as I know.

"AI can be a great help," he continued, "but so far it can't completely replace human developers and designers. Let's try it tomorrow and see how AI can help us."

New things you have learned today

- *Different kinds of fonts*—Serif, sans serif, and monospace are different types of fonts that you can use in your application. Serif is good for headers and book and documentation texts. Sans serif is used for menus, but also for headers and text. Monospace is used to demonstrate program code, filenames, and command examples.

- *Color codes*—Colors can be described using *hexadecimal* numbers, like `#a1d4c5`. They consist of three base colors: red, green, and blue. You can use these color codes to specify background, menu, header, and text colors for your web page.

- *Pictures have owners and licenses*—It's important to know that not all pictures you find on the internet can be used freely on your web pages. Pictures and photos have owners who decide how you can use their work. Often, you can use their pictures without paying them, but you should place an *attribution* on your page. It's a way to say "Thank you" for their work.

Code for this chapter

You can find the code for this chapter here: https://github.com/pavelanni/ pythonicadventure-code/tree/main/ch13.

Help from AI: Improving our code

## 14

In this chapter

- Erik and Emily ask AI for help
- AI gives code reviews
- AI writes comments and explains error messages
- AI explains itself
- AI gives other ideas on how to use AI

"Are you ready to get help from AI?" Simon asked Erik and Emily.

"Sure," Erik answered. "Is there a special AI site for developers?"

"There are several AI tools for developers," Simon said. "With some of them, you log in to the site and ask for help. You ask for a code review or for code explanations, for example. Other tools can be installed in your editor, and they help you write the code. You'll try those later, so today let's start with using a website. I have an account at ChatGPT—let's use it."

Simon opened a web page at https://chat.openai.com and entered his login name and password. They saw a simple page with a "Send a message . . ." prompt at the bottom.

ChatGPT PLUS

Send a message...

"Remember how I told you yesterday," he started, "that you have to explain precisely to AI what you want from it? It's not a chatbot where you can start with just 'How are you?' We want to get a code review for one of our functions, so we have to explain it that way. It's recommended that we tell the AI that it has to *act* as somebody. In this case, we'll ask it to act as a code reviewer. Then we'll tell it what we expect from it."

Simon started typing in the prompt window:

```
Act as a code reviewer. Your task  is to receive a function from me and
give me feedback on the code structure, syntax, any potential errors, and
improvements that can be made.
Here is my first function to review:
```

He stopped and said, "Let's begin with a simple function. For example, let's take the read_menu() function." He copied the function from the editor:

```
def read_menu(filename):
    f = open(filename)
    temp = f.readlines()
    result = []
    for item in temp:
        new_item = item.strip()
        result.append(new_item)

    return result
```

The AI started typing almost immediately:

Thank you for providing the code. Here's my review:

I've reviewed your read_menu *function and here is my feedback:*

- *Code structure—The overall structure of your code is simple and easy to understand. Good job!*
- *Syntax—The syntax is correct and follows Python conventions.*
- *Potential errors—The code lacks proper error handling, especially when it comes to file I/O operations. If the given filename does not exist or there's a permission problem, your code will raise an exception.*

- *Improvements:*
    - *You can use a* with *statement for opening the file, which automatically handles closing the file, even in cases of exceptions. This ensures that the file is properly closed after it has been used.*
    - *You can simplify the* for *loop using list comprehension, which makes your code shorter and more Pythonic.*

Here's an updated version of your function with the suggested improvements:

The AI created a separate window with Python code:

```
def read_menu(filename):
    try:
        with open(filename) as f:
            result = [item.strip() for item in f.readlines()]
    except FileNotFoundError:
        print(
        f"Error: The file '{filename}' could not be found.")
        result = []
    except PermissionError:
        print(f"Error: You do not have permission to read \
        the file '{filename}'.")
        result = []
    except Exception as e:
        print(f"An unexpected error occurred: {e}")
        result = []

    return result
```

After that, the AI added its explanations:

This version of the function includes error handling for file operations, uses a with *statement for handling the file, and contains a list comprehension for generating the result list.*

"Wow!" Emily and Erik said simultaneously.

Simon commented, "All valid points. Yes, using with open is a common practice when working with files. I didn't want to use it earlier because it would require additional explanation, and we were not ready for that yet. The try - except combination is also very common. In this case, if the menu file isn't found, or if you don't have permission to read it, then the program doesn't just crash with errors, but instead politely tells you what happened. It's a very good practice."

"What is *list comprehension*?" Erik asked.

"It's a special Python way to make for loops shorter. Look at the code the AI wrote:

```
result = [item.strip() for item in f.readlines()]
```

"It's a replacement for this loop:"

```
temp = f.readlines()
result = []
for item in temp:
    new_item = item.strip()
    result.append(new_item)
```

"Yes, it's shorter," Erik agreed, "but the loop is easier to understand."

"Right!" Simon said. "That's why we started with loops. They are easier to understand. Now that you know how it works, you can use the more compact version. I didn't understand list comprehensions myself at first. But I started using them more often, and now they're as easy to read as normal loops. And, as the AI correctly pointed out, it's more *Pythonic*. Oh, we can also ask the AI to explain that to us."

Simon typed:

```
Please explain, what is list comprehension in Python?
```

The AI answered:

List comprehension is a concise way to create a list in Python. It's a syntactic construct that allows you to create a new list by specifying the elements you want to include, usually based on an existing iterable (like a list, tuple, or range). List comprehensions are more concise and often faster than using a traditional for *loop and the* append() *method to build a list.*

The basic structure of a list comprehension is:

```
[expression for item in iterable if condition]
```

- expression: *An expression that determines the value of each item in the new list. It often involves the* item *variable.*
- item: *A temporary variable representing each element in the* iterable.
- iterable: *An iterable object (e.g., list, tuple, range) that you want to loop over.*
- if condition: *An optional condition that filters the elements from the iterable. Only elements for which the condition is true will be included in the new list.*

Here's a simple example that demonstrates how to use list comprehension:

```
# Traditional way to create a list of squares using a for loop
squares = []
for i in range(1, 6):
    squares.append(i**2)
print(squares)  # Output: [1, 4, 9, 16, 25]

# Using list comprehension to create the same list of squares
squares = [i**2 for i in range(1, 6)]
print(squares)  # Output: [1, 4, 9, 16, 25]
```

You can also use list comprehension with a condition. Here's an example that creates a list of even numbers between 1 and 10:

```
even_numbers = [x for x in range(1, 11) if x % 2 == 0]
print(even_numbers)  # Output: [2, 4, 6, 8, 10]
```

List comprehensions can make your code more concise and readable, especially for simple operations. However, for more complex operations or nested loops, it can become less readable, so it's essential to strike a balance between conciseness and readability.

"Let's ask the AI to help us with something else. When we wrote our code, we didn't write comments for it. That's not a good practice. You should add comments in your code to explain what you're doing. There might be somebody reading your code. Or, more often, you'll be reading it three months later. I guarantee you, if you don't comment your code, you'll be asking yourself 'What is this? Why did I write it this way? What did I mean by this?' Trust me, I'm speaking from experience," Simon said and smiled.

"So it's a good practice to comment your code. Usually, you do it yourself, but let's see if the AI can help us." He wrote the following in the prompt window:

```
Please add comments to the function you've just created.
```

The AI answered immediately:

Certainly! Here's the updated version of the function with added comments explaining each step:

```python
def read_menu(filename):
    """
    Reads the menu from a file and returns a list of items.

    :param filename: The name of the file containing the menu.
    :return: A list of menu items, with leading and trailing
    whitespaces removed.
    """
    try:
        # Open the file using 'with' to ensure it's properly
        # closed after use
        with open(filename) as f:
            # Read all lines from the file and remove whitespaces
            # using list comprehension
            result = [item.strip() for item in f.readlines()]
    except FileNotFoundError:
        # Handle the case when the file does not exist
        print(f"Error: The file '{filename}' could not be found.")
        result = []
    except PermissionError:
        # Handle the case when there is no permission to read
        # the file
        print(f"Error: You do not have permission to read \
        the file '{filename}'.")
        result = []
    except Exception as e:
```

```
        # Handle any other unexpected errors
        print(f"An unexpected error occurred: {e}")
        result = []

    return result
```

"This is really good!" Simon said. "Look: at the beginning of the function, it added a docstring. It's a special string that can be included in the documentation for your function. Then, for each exception, it added an explanation of what it means. I couldn't write better comments myself! Look at this example, and always add comments and docstrings to your code!"

"Oh, I thought AI would be doing it for us now," Erik said and smiled.

"Yes, AI can comment simple lines of code like exception handling," Simon answered, "but I'm sure pretty soon you'll start writing functions that aren't so simple, and even the smartest AI won't be able to explain them. Prepare to do it yourself, if you're going to write really original code."

"Can the AI help us with error messages?" Emily asked.

"Great idea!" Simon said. "Let try it—I'm sure it can explain some error messages. Erik, remember, at the very beginning you received your first error message?"

"Yes, I remember that you were very happy about it," Erik grumbled.

"Let me find it, I kept it in my notes. Here it is," Simon said. He entered the error message in the prompt window with his request:

```
Please explain the following Python error message:

Traceback (most recent call last):
  File "/home/erik/mu_code/menu.py", line 30, in <module>
    print("Main product: ", drinks[drink])
TypeError: list indices must be integers or slices, not str
```

The AI answered:

> *This error message means that you are trying to use a string as an index to access an element in a list, which is not allowed in Python. In the specific case of this error message, it seems that you are trying to access an element in the list* drinks *using a variable* drink *that contains a string. Here is an example code that would produce this error:*

```
drinks = ["coffee", "tea", "soda"]
drink = "coffee"
print("Main product: ", drinks[drink])
```

> *In this code,* drink *is a string variable that contains the value* "coffee". *When we try to access* drinks[drink], *Python raises a TypeError because the index must be an integer, not a string. To fix this error, you need to use an integer index to access the element in the list. For example, if you want to access the first element of the list, you would use* drinks[0]:

```
drinks = ["coffee", "tea", "soda"]
drink = 0
print("Main product: ", drinks[drink])
```

> *This would output* "Main product: coffee", *which is the first element of the* drinks *list.*

"It even knows what our application is about!" Erik exclaimed.

"Yes," Simon said. "We gave it just one error message, and it guessed what our program does.

"This is due to the way this AI program works," he added.

"And how does it work? Can you explain?" Emily asked.

"Well . . ." Simon started, "I'm not an expert in AI. I just read several articles. I'll try to explain how I understand it.

"People in AI companies—like OpenAI, which created ChatGPT—know how to *train* computers to understand human language and programs. For that, they give computers *tons* of texts and code. Then a special program, called a *model*—usually written in Python, by the way—analyzes all those texts and finds out which words are more often used with other words. Like in our case, the AI model figured out that often when people use the word 'drinks' they also use 'coffee', 'tea', and 'soda'. That's why it gave us an example that's very similar to our code.

"Also," Simon continued, "those models can calculate the so-called *text similarity* and compare different words and phrases. Then they can use those results to give you answers to questions like, 'What is related to Spain the same way Paris is related to France?' The model will calculate the 'distance' between 'Paris' and 'France' and then perform a math operation like this:

```
? = Spain + (Paris - France)
```

"It will get the answer 'Madrid'."

"Can I try it?" Emily asked.

"Yes, let's try it!" Simon said. "I read this explanation in several articles, but I never tried it myself."

Emily took the keyboard and entered in the prompt window:

```
What is related to Spain the same way Paris is related to France?
```

The AI answered:

> *Madrid is related to Spain the same way Paris is related to France. Both Madrid and Paris are the capital cities of their respective countries, Spain and France.*

"It works, indeed!" Simon said. "Let's ask it how it came to this answer."

Emily typed:

```
Can you please explain how you came to this answer?
```

The AI said:

> *Sure! I came to this answer by understanding the relationship between Paris and France. Paris is the capital city of France. So, the question is asking for something that has a similar relationship with Spain.*

Knowing that Madrid is the capital city of Spain, I identified that it has the same relationship with Spain as Paris has with France. Thus, I provided Madrid as the answer to the question. This type of reasoning is called analogical reasoning, where I find similarities between different pairs of items based on their relationships.

Simon added another question:

```
Did you use text similarity to find this relationship?
```

The AI answered:

As an AI language model, I didn't explicitly use text similarity to find the relationship between Paris and France, and then Madrid and Spain. Instead, I relied on my pre-existing knowledge and understanding of relationships between countries and their capital cities, which I have learned during my training on a large dataset of text.

However, text similarity techniques, like word embeddings, can help in finding relationships between words based on their context and usage. In this case, I used my knowledge and analogical reasoning to establish the relationship and provide the answer.

"How cool!" Simon said. "We can use AI to learn about AI! I know that people use AI for many other tasks to help them develop their programs. We tried writing comments, doing code reviews, and explaining error messages already. I wonder what else AI can help us with. Let's ask it!" He entered the following question:

```
We asked ChatGPT to help us with our Python project.
We tried writing comments, doing code reviews, explaining error messages
already.
What else can ChatGPT help us with?
```

The AI answered:

In addition to writing comments, doing code reviews, and explaining error messages, ChatGPT can also help you with various other aspects of your Python project, such as:

- *Generating code examples—ChatGPT can provide you with example code snippets to demonstrate how to use certain functions, libraries, or language features.*
- *Debugging—You can describe the problem you're facing, and ChatGPT can suggest potential solutions or ways to identify the root cause of the problem.*
- *Recommending libraries and tools—ChatGPT can recommend appropriate libraries or tools to use for specific tasks, based on its knowledge of popular and widely used resources in the Python ecosystem.*
- *Best practices and coding conventions—ChatGPT can provide guidance on best practices, coding conventions, and style guidelines to help you write clean, maintainable, and efficient Python code.*

- *Algorithm design—ChatGPT can help you understand or design algorithms, explaining their logic and providing examples of how they can be implemented in Python.*
- *Project structure—ChatGPT can provide advice on organizing your Python project, such as how to structure your directories, files, and modules, as well as guidance on package management and dependency handling.*

Remember that while ChatGPT can be helpful, it's not a replacement for thorough research and understanding of the concepts. Additionally, it's important to review the generated code or suggestions to ensure correctness and suitability for your specific project requirements.

"All great ideas!" Simon said. "I think we should try them together. Tomorrow, let's discuss all the possible ways to improve our application and make plans for the future," Simon said. "In the AI's answer, I think the last paragraph is very important. When people first see the code written by an AI, they start thinking that AI can do *everything* for them. But I played with it and noticed several times that not all the generated code works. You always have to review it and test it.

"Okay, back to our Coffee Shop application," he continued. "What else should we do with it?"

"You said I can open this application on my iPad," Erik said.

"Yes, it's possible, but we have to make a couple of minor changes. You're right, this application doesn't make a lot of sense if you can only use it on your computer. Tomorrow, I'll show you how to open it on your iPad or on your phone."

"Will we put it in the cloud?" Emily asked.

"Almost," Simon said. "For now, it will be in our own 'cloud' inside our home network. But you'll need to put it on the real cloud so it can be accessed from anywhere. Let's talk tomorrow."

New things you have learned today

- *AI can help you write good programs*—AI can help you write better code, explain error messages, fix bugs, and comment your code. AI can also give you ideas about program structure and useful tools and libraries.
- *AI doesn't replace the programmer*—AI can do a lot of interesting things, but it still needs human help to make working and useful applications. Not all code generated by an AI works without errors. You should always review and test it.
- *AI uses special programs called models*—AI uses language models to generate its answers. The models are *trained* on a huge amount of text, including Wikipedia, online articles, program code, and many others. Models can calculate relationships between words and sentences and build answers based on those calculations.

15

Next steps:
Plans for the future

"There's one minor thing left to do," Simon said, "before we can say we're done with this application. Remember, when we open our application, we see the 'Hello from Mu!' web page. I think it's time to replace that with our own home page."

"Of course!" Emily said. "We've already chosen our colors, and we found a good picture! I think we should just put the header 'Welcome to E&E Coffee Shop!' and add the picture we used on the order page."

"Yes, good idea," Simon said. "But don't forget the main purpose of the home page."

"What is the main purpose?" Erik asked.

"On any website or web application, you use your home page for *navigation*," Simon answered. "When people open your site, they should be able to quickly figure out what it does and how to use it. Take a look at your favorite coffee shop sites and tell me what you find there. Look for what they all have in common."

Emily and Erik searched for familiar companies and opened their websites in several tabs. After exploring them for some time, Erik said, "They all have a page called Menu. They have a Locations page or a Find a Store, where they show where to find their shops."

"You'll have to create one of those too, when you open several coffee shops," Simon commented.

"Yes," Erik said. He continued, "Also, they have rewards cards and gift cards. I think we need them too. And at the bottom, they usually have many smaller links. They have About Us, Contact Us, and others."

"You did great research," Simon said. "Now you can see what I mean by navigation. For now, we have only one page besides the home page, and that's our order page. I think we can just place a button on the home page that will lead to the order page."

"Like we did on the 'Here is your order' page?" Emily asked.

"Exactly!" Simon said. "You can just copy those three lines from the `print.html` page. Open the `templates/index.html` file, remove everything between the second line, with `block content`, and the last line, with `endblock`. Then insert what we just discussed: the title, the button, and the picture."

"Yes, now I know what to do," Emily said. They started working on the home page. After several minutes, Emily and Erik showed their home page to Simon:

> **Listing 15.1   `templates/index.html`: Create your home page**

```
{% extends "base.html" %}
{% block content %}

<h1>Welcome to E&E Coffee Shop</h1>

<form action="/order">
<input type="submit" value="New order" />
</form>

<img src="/static/img/8507631_3925457.jpg"
 alt="Coffee drinks" width="100%">
Image by <a href="https://www.freepik.com/free-vector/
take-away-coffee-coffee-mugs_8507631.htm">Freepik</a>

{% endblock %}
```

> ***Your Turn!*   Edit your home page**
>
> Open your `templates/index.html` file and make changes like Erik and Emily just did. Feel free to change the picture or the title.

"Looks good to me," he said. "Let's try it!

"Good. Now try to click New Order. It should open the order page," Simon said to Erik.

Erik did, and he saw the familiar order page with menus.

"Everything works!" he said. "Now we have a complete web application!"

"Simon," Emily started her question, "yesterday you said that we can use this application from our devices too. Can you show us how?"

"Yes, I want to try it on my iPad," Erik said.

"Yes, absolutely," Simon answered. "Erik, do you remember that this whole project started when you went to collect your orders with the iPad? And I told you that you can create a web application to use the iPad not only as a notebook?"

"Yes, I remember that," Erik said. "It was just a couple weeks ago," and he smiled.

"Okay, let's make it work on your iPad then," Simon said. "Let me explain what I'm going to do." He started drawing a diagram and explaining.

"When we run our application from the Mu editor, by default, it's available only from the computer where we're running it. That's why we used localhost, or the address 127.0.0.1, when using our application. Flask and the Mu editor do that to make sure we don't show our application to other computers and users while we're still working on it."

"That makes sense," Erik said. "It was not very pretty before we added fonts and pictures."

"Right," Simon said. "But now we're ready to use it on other devices, and we want to change that. Luckily, it's just one line in the Mu editor's configuration. After we make this change, all devices in our home network will be able to use it—if they have a browser, of course."

"Can I try it from my phone?" Emily asked.

"Yes, but you should connect to our home's network for that. Let me enter our Wi-Fi password," and Simon entered the password on Emily's phone.

"Here's the default configuration on the left," he continued his explanation. "We can access the application only from the computer it's running on. And here, on the right, we can access it from other devices.

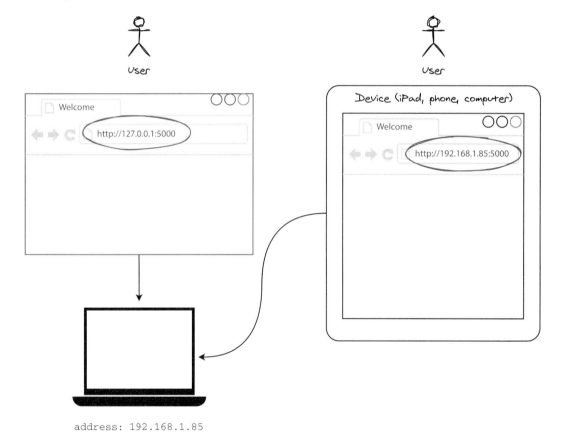

"Every computer has a *network address*. Your laptop, Erik, is connected to our home network. It has the address 192.168.1.85. Any other device in our network that wants to talk to it should use this address. If your computer wants to talk to *itself*, then it uses `127.0.0.1`."

"Can I try it now?" Erik asked.

"Wait, I have to make a change in the configuration. Remember, we're now showing our application to all devices in our home network. Of course, there aren't many devices connected, but we still want to make sure that our application is fully ready. In the future, we'll upload it to the cloud, and then *all computers in the world* will see it. We'd better make sure it works right and looks nice.

"Erik, do you see that little cogwheel in the bottom-right corner of the Mu editor?" Simon continued. "It usually means *settings* or *configuration*. Click it, please."

"Now select the `Python 3 Environment` tab, and add the following line at the end of the text there:"

```
FLASK_RUN_HOST=0.0.0.0
```

Erik did and saw the result.

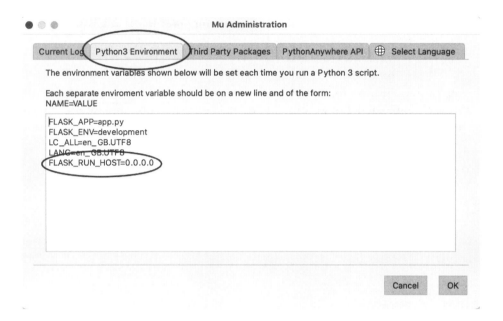

"Now click OK and restart the application."

Erik saved the configuration by clicking OK. He clicked Stop and then Run again in the editor.

Simon said, "Now look at the output in the bottom window. See this line `Running on all addresses`? That's exactly what we need. In the two lines below it, you'll see the addresses we can use to access the app. The first one is `127.0.0.1`, which we use all the time. The second one is your laptop's address in our home network. You should enter it in the browser on your iPad. And you, Emily, enter it on your phone. In this case, it's `http://192.168.1.85:5000`.

"Keep in mind that this address may change. For example, if you go to Emily's home with your laptop and connect to her home network, your laptop will get a different address. You'll see it in the output window, and, in Emily's home, you'll have to use that new address.

```
Running:
[31m[1mWARNING: This is a development server. Do not use it in a
instead. [0m
 * Running on all addresses (0.0.0.0)
 * Running on http://127.0.0.1:5000
 * Running on http://192.168.1.85:5000
[33mPress CTRL+C to quit [0m
 * Restarting with stat
 * Debugger is active!
 * Debugger PIN: 675-232-744
```

"Okay, now open this address on your devices, and show me what you've got on the order page."

Emily and Erik opened their devices and started typing.

"Got it!" Emily showed her phone.

"Looks great!" Simon said. "Erik, what's on your iPad?"
"Look!" Erik said.

"It works on both your devices, and it looks great," Simon said. "Remember, I told you that we're using the style sheets included with the Mu editor, and those sheets were designed to work on different devices. Here, we used your application on a MacBook, on an iPad, and on an Android phone, and it looks great on all of them. Even more, did you notice how our menus were rearranged to fit the page? That's the advantage of using the `normalize.css` and `skeleton.css` style sheets. We just added a couple of little changes with our `coffeeshop.css` style sheet."

"It's great that customers in our coffee shop can order drinks from their phones," Emily said. "But for that, they should be in the shop and connected to our network, right? Simon, can we place our application in the real cloud, so we can use it from anywhere? I'd love to show it to my friends at school."

"Sure, it's possible. Of course, it's a bit more complicated than just adding one string, like we just did. Usually, cloud services cost some money, but for simple projects like ours it's possible to find a free service. One of them is called PythonAnywhere. I know that they can host your Python application, but I haven't tried it myself. Give me some time, and I'll test it and give you the instructions."

NOTE You'll find the instructions for using PythonAnywhere on the book's companion website at https://pythonicadventure.com.

"But before we open the application to the whole world, let's talk about possible improvements. Erik, do you remember what we discussed when working with the database?"

"You said it would be good to include the time of the order in the database table," Erik said.

"Yes, right! Let's start a to-do list to plan our future improvements." He started writing in a text editor:

```
* Timestamps in orders
```

"We could remember each customer," Emily said, "and show them what they ordered last time."

"Good idea," Simon said. "But, in this case, we should create a unique name for each customer. We don't want to mix up two different customers whose names are Alex."

"What about our menus?" Erik asked. "When we run it on my laptop, we can edit the text files. But when we run it on the cloud, we can't edit the files, can we?"

"Yes, you're right, Erik," Simon said. "If we go to the cloud, everything should be done via a web browser. We'll need another page to edit menus. And don't forget that this page should be used only by shop managers."

"I see what you mean," Emily said. "We need passwords!"

"Right," Simon confirmed. "We need different *accounts* in our application. We'll have customer accounts, and we'll have barista accounts where they'll receive orders.

And we'll have shop manager accounts where they'll list orders, edit menus, and do other manager things."

"We need more pictures!" Emily said. "I mean, pictures of our products: all our flavors and toppings."

"What about promotions?" Erik asked. "Flavor of the week, or something like that. Simon, you said that we should know how many portions of flavors and toppings we used during a day or month. Is it possible to display this on the web?"

"Whoa, whoa, slow down please. I can't keep up with writing all your ideas down," Simon said and smiled. "Seriously, I like how we're brainstorming this. One of the main principles of brainstorming—and we use it often in our robotics club—is that criticizing ideas is not allowed. Everybody is welcome to bring the craziest ideas. We don't say, 'Oh, this will be impossible to implement'. We just collect *everything* and discuss it later."

"Then I'd like to add voice commands to our coffee shop," Erik said. "And a robotic arm to pour coffee and add flavors and toppings."

"Noted," Simon said.

"I think instead of passwords we should use face recognition," Emily said. "Passwords are boring. Imagine that a customer is entering the shop and we greet them and say, 'Hey, Max, are you going to have your usual vanilla with caramel?'"

"Great, noted too," Simon said. "Here's what I've collected so far." He showed his list to Emily and Erik:

```
* Timestamps in orders
* Remember each customer and what they ordered (create user accounts)
* Edit menus from the browser
* Accounts for shop managers, baristas, cashiers, customers
* List orders for a day, week, month; list all orders from a customer
* More pictures of our products
* Product promotions
* Reports: how many orders of each flavor and topping per day, week, month
* Voice commands
* Robotic arms for coffee, flavors, and toppings
* Face recognition for customers
```

"Also, don't forget the suggestions we received from the AI yesterday. Let me create another list," Simon said. He copied the answers from ChatGPT:

```
* Code examples: ask the AI to review all our functions and give suggestions
     for improvement
* Debugging: ask the AI to analyze our functions for potential bugs
* Recommend libraries and tools: ask the AI to give us suggestions
* Algorithm design: ask the AI to analyze our algorithms (we didn't use many
     yet)
* Project structure: ask the AI for suggestions on project structure
* Create tests for our functions (the AI didn't tell us yesterday, but I know
     people use it for tests)
```

"That's enough work for a whole year!" Simon said. "I'm afraid there's not enough space in the book to cover all that."

"What book?" Erik asked.

"Erik, don't you know?" Simon asked. "Our dad is writing a book about us—you, Emily, and me. The book is all about this coffee shop project and about how we developed it. He said he couldn't add more chapters to the book, so I'm afraid we'll have to continue our project online. I suggest we create a website and update it with our progress and the additional features that we develop. What do you think?"

"I like it!" Emily said. "It will be like a blog, right?"

"Yes, a blog! Maybe we should also add a GitHub repository, where we can keep all our programs and examples."

"Great!" Erik said. "I heard about GitHub—most developers keep their code there."

"And when we do that," Simon continued, "other people will be able to use our code, learn from it, and maybe add their own features to our application. Maybe they'll share their applications, and we'll help them too. This is how most projects are being developed these days."

"This is great! I'm in!" Emily said.

"Me too," Erik added.

"Great, let's continue on our own site then. I'll talk with Dad and we'll set it up together. See you tomorrow!" Simon said. He liked working on this project with Emily and Erik. He had learned a couple of new things, himself, because of the coffee shop project. "It's time to learn more about accounts, robotic arms, and face recognition so I can explain it to the kids," he was thinking.

NOTE Here is the site they created: https://pythonicadventure.com/. Come and find new ideas for your projects, troubleshooting hints, and more!

New things you have learned today

- *A home page*—The first page you see when you visit a website. Usually, it's used to tell visitors what they can find on the site.
- *A network address*—Each computer connected to a network has an address that allows other computers in the network to find it. If we want to access the web application on Erik's laptop, we need to know its network address.

Code for this chapter

You can find the code for this chapter here: https://github.com/pavelanni/pythonicadventure-code/tree/main/ch15.

appendix A
Ideas for your
first application

Creating a Coffee Shop application doesn't sound very attractive to you? Create something else! All the programming ideas and methods I discuss in this book are applicable to a lot of other projects. Just look around, and you'll get ideas for other applications.

Here are some examples:

Pizza place

This should be very similar to the Coffee Shop application. You could ask the customer the following:

- What is their main drink?
- What flavor do they want?
- What topping do they want?

You can give the customer a list of options for each question, and the customer chooses from the menu.

You could also ask the pizza place customers the following:

- What kind of crust do you want—thin or thick?
- What size—small, medium, or large?
- Which sauce do you want—red or white?
- What kind of pizza do you want—margherita, pepperoni, or veggie? (For ideas, go to your favorite pizza place and see what they have.)
- What additional toppings do you want to add?

Ice cream shop

Go to your favorite ice cream shop, and watch how they prepare your order. What do they ask you? What options do they give you? Those will be in your application's menus.

Most likely, they will ask you the following:

- What type of cone—sugar, waffle, or cake?
- How many scoops?
- Which flavors?
- Any toppings?

Here, it's slightly different from the coffee shop. After you ask "How many scoops?" you'll have to ask that many times for the flavor for each scoop. Think about it: how would you do it in Python?

Here's a hint: There is a `range()` function in Python that can be used in a `for` loop. We used it in our menus. Try to use it to ask about the ice cream flavor the exact number of times.

LEGO minifigures

Perhaps you have a good collection of LEGO minifigures and their parts, and you want to help your friends build something new. What questions will you ask them, and what options will you give them? The following are some examples:

- *Choose the head*—smiley face, sunglasses face, face with a beard
- *Choose the headwear*—dark hair, blond hair, hard hat, police hat
- *Choose the torso*—mechanic, police officer, shirt with tie, t-shirt
- *Choose the legs*—blue jeans, green shorts, brown cargo pants
- *Choose the accessory*—a sword, a radio, a hammer, a magnifying glass

You can add special conditions to your application. For example, if your friend has chosen a police hat, they can't choose a baseball bat as an accessory. Think about adding this condition to your menus.

What about choosing parts at random? That might create some funny minifigures. How would you add a random option to your menu? How would you implement it?

Here's a hint: There is a module called `random` in Python. You should import it with the `import` statement at the beginning of your program and use the `choice()` function. You can give that function a list of choices, and it chooses one of them randomly. The next time you call it, the function randomly chooses something else (or maybe the same item—it's random!). For example, create the following short program and run it. In this program, we ask Python five times to randomly choose an item from a list of three types of hair.

Listing A.1 `choice.py`

```
import random

for _ in range(5):
    print(random.choice(["dark hair", "blond hair", "red hair"]))
```

Run the program as `python choice.py`, and you'll see something like this:

```
blond hair
red hair
blond hair
blond hair
dark hair
```

Of course, your list will be different and will probably have 5 *other* random choices in a different order.

Other project ideas

Do you have other project ideas? Please share them in the liveBook forum: https://livebook.manning.com/book/a-pythonic-adventure/discussion.

appendix B
How to install the Mu editor and Python environment

In this appendix, I'll explain how to install Python on your computer. The easiest way is to install a programming editor that contains Python. I recommend you install the Mu editor. I use it in this book, so it will be easy to follow the book's dialogues and instructions if you're using the same editor.

I'll also give you links to other ways to install Python—feel free to try them too.

Mu

Follow these steps to install Mu:

1 In your web browser, open the Mu editor's web page: https://codewith.mu/.

Code with Mu: a simple Python editor for beginner programmers.

2 Click Download (the green button). You'll see the Download Mu page.

Download Mu

The simplest and easiest way to get Mu is via the official installer for Windows or Mac OSX (we no longer support 32bit Windows). We also have an experimental AppImage for Linux users running on Intel based hardware.

The current recommended version is Mu 1.2.0. We advise people to update to this version via the links for each supported operating system. All previous beta versions of Mu can be downloaded from here.

Windows Installer

Download   Instructions

Mac OSX Installer

Download   Instructions

Linux AppImage Package (Experimental)

Download   Instructions

3 Click Download for your operating system. You browser will download the installation file for your operating system as follows:

- For Windows it will be an `.msi` file.
- For macOS it will be a `.dmg` file.
- For Linux it will be an `.AppImage` file.

4 Click Instructions for your operating system and follow the instructions.

5 Open Mu as you normally open applications in your operating system. You're ready to work on your project!

You can also use the Mu editor to program microcontrollers and build robots, but that's a topic for another book.

Thonny

Thonny is another great Python editor created with beginners in mind. You can find it here: https://thonny.org/.

On the first page, you'll find the installers for Windows, macOS, and Linux. For Windows, download the `.exe` file and run it. For macOS, download the `.pkg` file and install it. For Linux, run the command provided in the instructions.

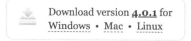

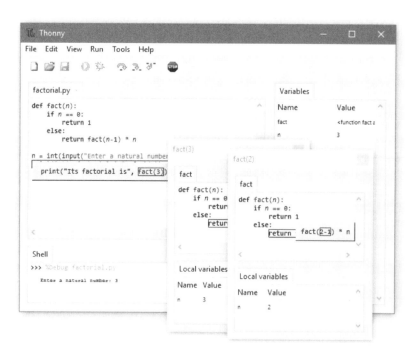

After you've installed the application, start it and explore its settings. You can choose a color theme from a dozen options, the editor and terminal fonts, and many other options.

Thonny has a very helpful feature called Assistant. In the Options menu, you can configure it to start each time when there is a warning in your code. It also starts when your program shows an error. Assistant gives you several suggestions about what could be wrong with your code. Try to make a minor mistake in your code (a typo in a variable name, for example), and then run the program. You'll see Assistant in action.

Python

Both of the preceding editors include Python in their installation packages. But, for some reason, you may want to install Python separately.

If you are on macOS or Linux, your operating system already has Python installed. Most likely, it's not the latest version of Python, but that's not a problem: all the programs we develop in this book will work with Python versions starting from 3.5. There's no need to install anything on these operating systems—at least, not for this book.

If you're on Windows, you'll have to go to the official Python site and download the installer from there: https://www.python.org/downloads/windows/.

Please read the notes carefully and choose the right Python version for your Windows version.

Python Releases for Windows

- Latest Python 3 Release - Python 3.11.0

Stable Releases

- Python 3.11.0 - Oct. 24, 2022

  Note that Python 3.11.0 *cannot* **be used on Windows 7 or earlier.**

  - Download Windows embeddable package (32-bit)
  - Download Windows embeddable package (64-bit)
  - Download Windows embeddable package (ARM64)
  - Download Windows installer (32-bit)
  - Download Windows installer (64-bit)
  - Download Windows installer (ARM64)

- Python 3.9.15 - Oct. 11, 2022

  Note that Python 3.9.15 *cannot* **be used on Windows 7 or earlier.**

  - No files for this release.

- Python 3.8.15 - Oct. 11, 2022

  Note that Python 3.8.15 *cannot* **be used on Windows XP or earlier.**

  - No files for this release.

- Python 3.10.8 - Oct. 11, 2022

  Note that Python 3.10.8 *cannot* **be used on Windows 7 or earlier.**

Another way to install Python on Windows is to open a PowerShell window and type python. Windows will suggest the right version of Python to install. You just have to accept it.

index

V

values 152
  in HTML 125–126
  in Python dictionaries 76
  passing from web forms to programs 139
variables 11–12, 15–16, 23–24, 125, 152
  in HTML 125, 140–141
  naming 36
  returning 37
  visibility of 37

W

web browser, opening files in 124
web forms, passing values to program from 139
Web mode, Mu editor 117
web service 142
weight, of fonts 170
while loop 50, 79, 84